BE AN ARMCHAIR DETECTIVE

MURDER AT THE CHESSBOARD

BE AN ARMCHAIR DETECTIVE

MURDER
AT THE
CHESSBOARD

&

43 other perplexing
whodunit puzzlers to test
your crime-solving skills

BLACK DOG
& LEVENTHAL
PUBLISHERS

This edition contains the texts of the following original editions. They have been reorganized and reset for this volume. This edition was originally published in separate volumes under the titles:

Great Quicksolve Whodunit Puzzles © 1998 by James Richard Sukach
Baffling Whodunit Puzzles © 1996 by James Richard Sukach
Whodunit Puzzles ©1997 by James Richard Sukach
Quicksolve Whodunit Puzzles ©1995 by James Richard Sukach
Crimebusters © 2000 by Stanley Smith
Five-Minute Whodunits © 1997 by Stanley Smith
Almost Perfect Crimes © 1995 by Hy Conard
Almost Perfect Murders © 1997 by Hy Conard
Inspector Forsooth's Whodunits © 1998 by Derrick Niederman
Baker Street Puzzles © 1992 by Tom Bullimore/Knight Features
Puzzles of Deduction © 1997 by Tom Bullimore

Library of Congress Cataloging-in-Publication Data

Murder at the Chessboard: & 43 other perplexing whodunit puzzlers to test your crime-solving skills/ edited by P. T. Houdunitz

p   cm.
ISBN 1-57912-162-4
1   Puzzles 2.Detective and mystery stories I. Houdunitz, P. T., 1974-

GV1507.D4 M87 2001
793.73—dc21

Book design: Edward Miller
Printed in the United States of America

Published by
Black Dog & Leventhal Publishers, Inc.
151 West 19th Street
New York, New York 10011

Distributed by
Workman Publishing Company
708 Broadway
New York, New York 10003

h g f e d c b

CONTENTS

CRYPTIC CASES

CURIOUS QUANDARIES

INTRODUCTION

Are you an amateur sleuth? Now you can join the ranks of the great detectives and solve these challenging puzzles, tackling everything from backyard thefts to international murder cases.

The first section, Puzzling Predicaments, will get you started with short mysteries and puzzles to warm up your natural deduction skills. You will join forces with Dr. J.L. Quicksolve, a professor of criminology who now works as a crime consultant, and with Thomas P. Stanwick, a British amateur logician. In the next section, Cryptic Cases, you will find more challenging mysteries with a mosaic of clues that you will need to piece together. Here you will meet Inspector Foorsooth, who tested his mysteries online. The questions and answers that follow each case are taken directly from those online solving sessions, to help point you in the right direction. Finally, for the advanced sleuth, Curious Quandaries offers complex mysteries you might need to read more than once. These feature evidence files and an analysis of the evidence to help you evaluate the crime scene. Think you know whodunit? Check the solutions at the end of the book.

Ready for fun? Take your time, consider each clue and remember, everyone is a suspect!

Good Luck!

P.T. Houdunitz

PUZZLING
PREDICAMENTS

COUNTRY KILLING

Jim Sukach

Dr. J.L. Quicksolve sped along in his bright yellow VW Beetle. He looked at the sun beginning to set to his right across the expanse of corn growing in the fields. Sun and corn belong together, he thought, out here in this beautiful country atmosphere but not murder.

Sergeant Rebekah Shurshot met Dr. Quicksolve at the door of the small house nestled between the huge oak trees, a small oasis in the sea of cornfields. The front door, hanging to the floor from one hinge, was the first sign something was amiss. The second was the blanket-covered body on the floor. Dr. Quicksolve had to step around it.

Sergeant Shurshot led him through the mass of overturned furniture and broken lamps into the small dining area. Sergeant Shurshot introduced Dr. Quicksolve to Spinner Webb, the nephew of the deceased.

"My aunt had not been feeling well," Spinner said. "She had been depressed ever since her dog, Spookum, disappeared." Dr. Quicksolve noticed the curtains were drawn, as if the elderly lady had wanted to live in the misery of darkness while she mourned. "She didn't answer when I knocked," Mr. Webb continued. "I pushed on the door. It opened

barely an inch, stopped by the chain lock. I shouted for her, but I got no answer. I could see inside enough to tell the house had been ransacked. I was worried, so I slammed my shoulder against the door and broke in. I came inside and looked around. I stumbled over my aunt's body in the dark. That scared me half to death!"

"There is one window open in the back," Sergeant Shurshot said. "The screen has been cut."

"The murderer must have escaped through that window," Webb said.

"You weave quite a story, Mr. Webb," Dr. Quicksolve said.

Q. Why did Dr. Quicksolve doubt Spinner Webb's story?

A. pg. 203

SPEEDY GETAWAY

Jim Sukach

Dr. J.L. Quicksolve was driving west on Eisenhower Boulevard, heading out of town. He got a call on his cellular phone. It was Officer Longarm reporting a bank robbery. Dr. Quicksolve pulled his yellow VW Beetle to the side of the road while he listened to Officer Longarm.

The bank had been robbed by one gunman. Witnesses said the robber wore a shaggy beard and a baseball cap, and he had long hair tied in a ponytail. He said nothing. He handed the clerk a note demanding money and lifted his left hand just enough to show the gun. He ran out the door with a large bag of money and jumped into a waiting getaway car.

Dr. Quicksolve asked for a description of the car "It was unique," officer Longarm said. "It was a white Jaguar convertible. They had the top down, and the robber jumped in over the door. Witnesses said there was a large dent in the driver's door. Otherwise, it looked as good as new. No one got a license number."

"That's an unusual getaway car," Dr. Quicksolve said. "Criminals usually don't want to be so conspicuous. They want to blend in and not get noticed."

"The getaway car headed west, but it could have turned anywhere," Officer Longarm said.

Dr. Quicksolve looked down the road ahead and saw two women waiting on the side of the road at a bus stop. One woman was sitting on a suitcase as they waited for a bus. Dr. Quicksolve slowly drove up to the bus stop and rolled down the passenger window of his car to talk to the women.

"Did you see any unusual cars drive by here recently?"

he asked. "Any convertibles?"

"Yes, we did," one of the women said. "We saw a white Jaguar driving like crazy—headed west. The top was down, and it had a dent in the driver's door. It must be long gone by now."

Dr. Quicksolve thanked the women, pulled up half a block, and spoke into his phone. "Officer Longarm, I have two suspects."

Q. Why did Dr. Quicksolve suspect the two women?

A. pg. 203

BACKYARD BANDIT

Jim Sukach

Dr. J.L. Quicksolve arrived at the home of Mr. and Mrs. John Mark. Mrs. Mark came to the door and let him in. She and Mr. Mark explained that they had been robbed while they were away for the weekend. They said their neighbor had seen the burglar. Dr. Quicksolve asked to talk with the neighbor, Mr. Dare.

John Mark led Dr. Quicksolve out the back door. Mr. Dare was on a ladder on the other side of an eight-foot hedge that separated the two backyards. John introduced Dr. Quicksolve and Mr. Dare. "Dr. Quicksolve would like to ask you a few questions," John said.

"I told the police officer everything, but, sure, I don't mind," Mr. Dare said.

"Just tell me what you saw, Mr. Dare," Quicksolve said.

"Well, it happened this morning. I was mowing the grass here in my backyard. I heard a funny noise over here, and I saw a man at John's back door, picking the lock. He got inside pretty quickly. I ran into my house and called the police. Just before they got here I saw him run out the back door carrying a large box. The police were

just a few minutes too late."

"Could you describe the man?" Dr. Quicksolve asked.

"Sure. The police have the description," Mr. Dare said.

"I guess it doesn't really matter, unless

you described yourself," Dr. Quicksolve said.

 Why does Dr. Quicksolve suspect Mr. Dare?

 pg. 204

PUZZLE NO.1

Professor Moriarty's three partners in crime listened as he explained how they would rob Mansfield Hall.

"Have you got all that?" said Moriarty finally. "It's important that we rob the four rooms in sequence before making our escape . . . What's the sequence Scarface?"

"Eh . . . The kitchen, study, games room and the library,"said Scarface.

Moriarty shook his head, "You got two right," he said.

"Is it the library, games room, kitchen, study?" said Fingers.

"You only got one right,"snapped Moriarty. "How about you, Knuckles?"

"I've been paying attention, Boss," said Knuckles. "It's the kitchen, games room, study and library," he said confidently.

"I don't believe it!" screamed Moriarty. "You've got them all wrong!"

Can you give the correct order?

 A. pg.237

THE CASE OF THE BULGONIAN SPY

Stan Smith

The ducks in James Park eagerly accepted the bread crumbs Thomas P. Stanwick offered as he sat on a bench chatting with his old friend Inspector Gilbert Bodwin. Stanwick was in London for a week to relax and attend a symposium on logic education. He and Bodwin were discussing crime, as usual.

"Then there's my spy case," remarked Bodwin. "The Yard is assisting DI5 (the old MI5, like your CIA, of course) in recovering stolen Ministry of Defence plans for a submarine firing sequence scrambler. We've established that they were taken by someone at the embassy of the Free Democratic People's Republic of North Bulgonia, which has for

years been angling for military technology to use against the genuinely free Republic of South Bulgonia."

"Submarine plans?" Stanwick looked puzzled. "Aren't both countries landlocked?"

"Yes, but they share a large lake, and maintain freshwater sub fleets."

Stanwick laughed. "And how were the plans taken?"

"A senior Defence official, Warren Perry, very carelessly took away a copy of the plans and left them exposed in the bar of a hotel, where they disappeared. He has since been reprimanded. We believe that the thief was one of two North Bulgonian embassy employees, Vlado Impalus or Boris Gulkovo. Both were in the bar that evening."

"Indeed? Please go on."

Bodwin grunted and pulled out his official notebook. "We've interviewed the bartender, the waitress, the hotel concierge, and several others," he said. "Perry arrived at the bar at 6:30 P.M. with a woman, took a table, and ordered cocktails. They sat at drinks for an hour and a half, then the woman left. Perry opened his briefcase and worked for an hour. Then his phone beeper went off, and he was gone for a quarter of an hour answering it. Fifteen minutes after his return, he noticed the plans missing and raised the alarm."

"Impalus arrived at the bar with a friend half an hour after Perry. They drank gin-and-tonics at a table for an hour and a quarter until the friend left. A quarter of an hour later, Impalus went to the gents', returning after another quarter of an hour. Sometime in the next half-hour, he left."

"The other one, Gulkovo," Bodwin continued, "arrived at the bar alone half an hour after Impalus arrived, took a table, and drank a whiskey and soda. After three-quarters of an hour, he went to the gents' for a quarter of an hour. A quarter of an hour after his return, he went to the lounge, bought a paper, and read it there for half an hour. Then he returned to the bar briefly, picked up his coat, and left."

"Hmm." Stanwick threw his remaining bread crumbs into the pond, where several ducks swarmed upon them. "Is Perry sure that the plans were in his case when he arrived?"

"Yes. He saw them when he began working on his papers. We have ample evidence, incidentally, that he is guilty only of incompetence, not espionage."

"In that case," said Stanwick, standing up and stretching, "the identity of the spy is clearly deducible. How about some lunch?"

 Who is the spy?

A. pg. 204

FAKE OUT

Jim Sukach

Sergeant Rebekah Shurshot and Officer Longarm were happy to have company for their overnight stakeout when Dr. Quicksolve asked if he could join them. They had spent another night hidden among the trees in a park on the edge of town watching a small farmhouse. A light snow fell, covering the ground and creating a beautiful scene and slippery roads. The farmhouse was the home of the girl-friend of Wallace Webb. Webb, alias Spider, was a recent escapee from State Prison. The night was as uneventful as the previous four, but at least they had the pleasure of swapping stories with the famous dectective and their good friend, Dr. J.L. Quicksolve.

They finally got something worth their attention as Sergeant Shurshot was driving Dr. Quicksolve home. A nearby party store had been robbed. The store owner did not have a good description of the robber's car, but he did know what direction it had taken. Sergeant Shurshot turned on her flashing lights and sped down the narrow country road. "There isn't likely to be anyone out here this early but the robber," she said to Dr. Quicksolve, who sat beside her.

The road was long and straight with nothing but trees on either side for miles. The sergeant slowed as they approached a car on the side of the road. The trunk was up, and a man was just pulling his jack from under the car. Sergeant Shurshot sped by as Dr. Quicksolve said, "Our first suspect."

"He was putting the jack away. He must have changed his tire already, meaning he's been there too long to be our suspect," Sergeant Shurshot explained, obviously proud of her logic. "I'll call Officer Longarm and have him check the guy out to be sure," she said, reaching for the microphone on the dashboard.

A few minutes later Officer Longarm called back over the radio. He said he was with the car on the side of the road behind them. He checked the tire in the trunk. It was flat, so the driver seemed to have a good alibi. He was surprised, though, that the man had no identification.

"I have a question about the tire," Dr. Quicksolve said.

Q. What question? What did the detective suspect?

A. pg. 205

WOOF WOOF BANG! BANG!

Jim Sukach

The body of Shirley Stonedead lay face down on the stairs. One arm stretched up to the stair above her head. It almost looked as if she had fallen asleep on the stairs, except for the three bullet holes in her back. At the bottom of the steps lay a pit bull terrier. It had taken two bullets to stop the dog.

The police photographer was taking pictures as a tall man in a flashy suit, Barrie Scarrie, talked to Dr. J.L. Quicksolve and Sergeant Rebekah Shurshot. The long scar on the man's face seemed to make a smile impossible. "I had an early appointment with Miss Stonedead. She owed me money. I came to pick it up," Barrie said. "As I was just about to push the doorbell, I heard a dog bark and two shots. Then I heard a noise in the back of the house, and a car came backing out of the driveway and took off. I didn't see the driver, and I didn't recognize the car. The door of the house was unlocked, so I went in. I saw Miss Stonedead and her dead dog. I called the police. That's all I know."

"Have you known Miss Stonedead long?" Dr. Quicksolve asked.

"Yes, I have. I used to work here. I was her bodyguard," Barrie explained.

Dr. Quicksolve and Sergeant Shurshot stepped aside to listen to what Officer Longarm had found out. "The back door was broken open.

A safe upstairs was jimmied open too. "It's empty," Officer Longarm said. "It had to be a burglar. Did Mr. Scarrie give you a description of the suspect?" Officer Longarm asked Sergeant Shurshot.

"No," Sergeant Shurshot answered, "but I imagine he has a picture of the murderer in his wallet." Dr. Quicksolve chuckled at her little joke.

 Q. What did Sergeant Shurshot mean?

A. pg. 205

PUZZLE NO.2

In the hope of trapping Professor Moriarty, Sherlock Holmes disguised himself as a street trader. He set up a stall in the market place and began to sell his wares to the public. Later he was visited by Dr. Watson.

"Has Moriarty appeared yet?" asked Watson.

"Not yet," replied Holmes. "The only customers I've had came together. They were two fathers and two sons. Between them they spent £3 at the stall. Surprisingly, they all spent exactly the same amount."

Watson glanced at Holmes. "If they spent £3 between them, Holmes, they couldn't have spent the same!"

But they had. Just how much had each of them spent?

A. pg.237

TALE OF THE GENEROUS RAJAH

Stan Smith

An armchair in the reading room of the Baskerville Public Library proved too comfortable a place for Thomas P. Stanwick at four o'clock on a warm afternoon. His eyes slid closed, his head slumped to his chest, and the book slipped from his fingers to the floor.

The head librarian, who had seen these symptoms before, walked quietly over to the amateur logician and gently shook his shoulder.

"Mr. Stanwick! You haven't fallen asleep, have you, sir?" she asked.

Stanwick snapped to alertness.

"What?" he said. "Oh, hello, Mrs. Mitten. Good

Lord, I wasn't snoring, was I?"

"No, no. I caught you in time."

"Thank you." Stanwick sheepishly picked up the book. "It's no reflection on what I was reading. Have you seen the memoirs of Morton Henry Stanley? He was a British explorer who traveled from Bombay across the Thar Desert to the northern reaches of India in the early 1800's."

"No, I don't think I've heard the name." Intrigued, the librarian sat down in the chair beside Stanwick's and examined the book closely.

"Stanley had many interesting adventures," Stanwick went on. "In one, he missed an excellent chance of gaining a large fortune in precious stones."

"Do go on," the librarian said.

Stanwick settled back in his chair and toyed with the tip of his droopy mustache.

"Well, as you probably know," he recounted, "India in those days had many independent kingdoms, or raji, each ruled by a fierce rajah. During one of his journeys, Stanley was captured by one of

those rajahs. The rajah found his prisoner to be a fascinating conversationalist. (Stanley was a gifted linguist and knew several Indian dialects.) They discussed local politics and world events, and played many games of chess.

"That night the rajah presided over an elaborate dinner, which was, according to his custom, to have been followed by the execution of the trespasser. The rajah, however, announced that he would give Stanley an opportunity to leave the raj unharmed and even wealthy.

"Three large chests were brought in to the center of the dining hall. Each was lavishly bound and secured by a huge lock. A besotted servant then stumbled in carrying three signs, one picturing a diamond, another picturing a ruby, and the third picturing an emerald. The fellow first put the emerald sign on the first trunk. After a confused pause, he then took that sign off the first trunk and put it on the second trunk. Finally, after some fumbling, he put the diamond sign on the first trunk and the ruby sign on the third trunk. Then he staggered out.

"'You must forgive my servant,' laughed the rajah, turning to his guest of honor. 'He has taken a little too much hashish today. I am afraid that in none of his attempts did he succeed in putting the correct sign on the correct chest. Nonetheless, one chest does contain diamonds, another contains rubies, and another emeralds.'

"'Each chest has a rather complicated lock. Here is a golden lockpick. I will give you five minutes to open one of the chests. Seeing its contents should enable you to divine the contents of all three chests. If you succeed in divining this, you may have all three chests and their contents, and safe passage to the border. If you fail, I fear I must proceed with the execution. You may begin.'

"Stanley needed no further prompting. Snatching up the lockpick, he hurried over to the three chests, paused briefly, and then began furious-ly picking at the lock of the middle chest, the one with the emerald sign. As the rajah chuckled quietly, Stanley muttered to himself and wrestled with the lock. Beads of sweat glistened on his forehead as the rajah called time. With a curse, Stanley flung the pick to the ground and glared at the still impregnable lock.

"The rajah laughed heartily at the spectacle of the explorer's fury and frustration."

"'Such a pity!' he exclaimed. 'I fear that the lock was too stubborn for you.'

"'Just tell me what is in one of these chests, good rajah,' said Stanley, 'and I will indeed tell you what is in the other two.'

"'I am sure you could, my friend, replied the

rajah. 'But fear not. You have entertained me well today, so I will spare your life and reward you for your company.'

"The rajah then made good on his word by giving

our relieved hero a small bagful of precious stones and a mounted escort to the border of the raj."

Stanwick grinned slyly. Mrs. Mitten, who had a weakness for tales of adventure in exotic lands, remained lost in thought for moment.

"It's a shame that he couldn't open the lock," she said at last. "I think I see how he could then have deduced the contents of all three chests, if all the signs were put on wrong."

"Quite true!" said Stanwick with a laugh. "Poor Stanley, however, was not quite astute enough to guess the real cause of the rajah's amusement. If only the brave explorer had been a little more alert, he might have realized that he had the power to 'divine' the contents of all three chests without touching the lockpick at all."

 How could Stanley have done this?

A. pg. 206

THE MYSTERIOUS WOMAN

Jim Sukach

The mysterious woman was a jewel thief who attended fancy parties and usually left with the jewels of the host or special guests. She was a master of disguises and rarely looked the same. She had managed to slip away time and again, and now she was back in town.

This time Lieutenant Rootumout and Dr. Quicksolve were ready for her. Dr. Quicksolve's friend Fred Fraudstop was to have a lavish party to celebrate his purchase of a spacious new home and to display his collection of fine art . Word was spread about the large and valuable collection of jewels Lucy Looker had left in his safe while she was out of town. Dr. Quicksolve, Lieutenant Rootumout, and several other police officers would be at the party.

Would she be lured by the jewels, or would she sense a trap?

The party was lavish, indeed. The spacious room was filled with well-dressed people talking happily and enjoying the drinks and hors d'oeuvres brought around by smiling servers.

"You both have seen her before?" Fred Fraudstop asked Dr. Quicksolve and Lieutenant Rootumout as they looked over the crowd of people.

"Yes," Dr. Quicksolve answered, "but that doesn't mean a lot. I know she looked about your height at that last party. I might recognize her walk. But remember, she's a master of disguises. She isn't likely to look like she did the last time we saw her. The best thing we can do is to look for strangers. I know most of the people you invited. Everyone else is a suspect."

"I'm going upstairs to the library, where the paintings are on display. I'm sure people will have questions," Fred said.

Dr. Quicksolve and Lieutenant Rootumout watched Fred work his way through the party crowd and climb the stairs. "See anyone suspicious?" Lieutenant Rootumout asked Dr. Quicksolve. Just then a beautiful woman began climbing the stairs across the room. Both men watched her closely until she reached the top of the stairs, where she turned to the right, out of sight. Dr. Quicksolve knew the house. There were only two rooms in the direction she turned—the library, where the paintings were displayed, and Fred's bedroom, where the jewels were locked in his safe.

"That's her," Dr. Quicksolve said as he began to work his way through the crowd. Many people recognized him as he passed, and he had to say a few words of greeting to avoid being rude, which slowed his progress and increased his anxiety and sense of déjà vu.

He eventually reached the stairs and climbed them quickly, with Lieutenant Rootumout right behind, hand on his pistol. Looking into the bedroom, they saw the open safe.

"She didn't come downstairs," Lieutenant Rootumout said.

Dr. Quicksolve checked the windows, which they had nailed shut to prevent her escape. "Look around," he said.

"Here!" Lieutenant Rootumout picked up something from behind the door. It was a small purse, overflowing with jewels.

"She's still up here," Dr. Quicksolve said, leaving the bedroom and entering the library.

There were three people in the library quietly looking at the paintings with their backs to Dr. Quicksolve and Lieutenant Rootumout. There was Fred Fraudstop and another man an inch shorter than Fred, but with more hair. The third person was a woman a little taller than either man.

"Arrest the man," Dr. Quicksolve said.

Q. Why the man?

A. pg. 207

STANWICK VISITS SCOTLAND YARD

Stan Smith

"Stanwick, my dear fellow," exclaimed Bodwin, "you couldn't possibly have chosen a better moment to come to London."

"London in April hasn't quite the reputation of  the French capital," replied Thomas P. Stanwick with a grin as he sat down. "Still, I'm always glad to be back."

The amateur logician had stopped at Scotland Yard to visit his old friend Inspector Gilbert Bodwin.

Stanwick was in London for a week to attend a Churchill Society dinner in Pall Mall.

"I expect this must be a particularly busy time for you," Stanwick continued, "with the foreign ministers' conference only a week away."

Bodwin leaned forward intently across his desk. "It is indeed, and that's why I'm glad to have a chance to talk with you."

"Oh?" Stanwick finished lighting his pipe and peered at Bodwin curiously through a cloud of smoke.

"Yes, and the Prime Minister is furious at the breach in security. Some important state papers were taken from a safe at the Foreign and Commonwealth Office two nights ago, at about nine-thirty. From the way it was done, we know the thief had to have known the combination of the safe.

"We have three suspects. They are all clerks in the FCO: James Malcolm, Samuel

Hickory, and William Dell. Each knows the combination as part of his duties."

Stanwick, full of interest, absentmindedly fingered a tip of his mustache.

"Of course you've questioned them," he said. "Just what accounts do they give of their whereabouts on the evening of the theft?"

Bodwin flipped open a notebook. "Malcolm says he went to the theatre with his wife that evening."

The inspector produced four scraps of paper, which Stanwick recognized as the halves of two torn tickets.

"He showed us these from his jacket pocket," Bodwin went on. "As you can see, they are for that evening's 8:00 o'clock performance of 'Coningsby' at the Disraeli Playhouse in Southwark. The play lasted until ten, and the ushers say no one left early. The Malcolms live in Chiswick and say they travelled to and from the theatre in their own car.

"Hickory maintains that he was engrossed in a darts tournament at his neighborhood pub from eight until eleven that night. That's the Sacred Cow in St. John's Wood. I have statements here from several of the regulars, all of whom confirm that Hickory was there the whole time."

"Does he often play darts there?" asked Stanwick.

The regulars say he stops by about twice a week for an evening pint," Bodwin replied, "but he hardly ever plays darts."

"How about Dell?"

"He's the only one without an alibi that we could readily verify. He lives alone and says he spent the whole evening watching television. He told my sergeant the plots of all that evening's BBC1 Programs, but he's still our prime susspect. There just isn't anything solid to go on."

"Does he also live in town?"

Bodwin nodded. "Small flat in Belgrave Road. Any suggestions? The P.M. will want my head on a platter if we don't nab our man."

Stanwick laughed and languidly stood up.

"I'm ready for a bite of lunch," he said. "If you'll join me in a stroll to the little pub I saw down the street, I'll be glad to tell you the identity of the thief."

 Who stole the documents?

A. pg. 208

PUZZLE NO.3

Sherlock Holmes and Dr. Watson were relaxing by the fire in the study of 221b Baker Street. Holmes was puffing on his favourite pipe while Watson was reading the Times. Suddenly, Watson

glanced over the top of the newspaper and looked directly at Holmes. "When is your birthday, Holmes?" he asked.

"You tell me, Watson," Holmes replied with a smile. "The day before yesterday I was thirty two, and next year I will be thirty five!"

"Impossible!" snapped Watson.

But Holmes was right. Can you tell what day of the year Holmes celebrated his birthday?

 pg.237

DEATH OF A CON MAN

Stan Smith

Thomas P. Stanwick was engrossed in revising some notes at his desk late one spring afternoon when the doorbell rang. He opened the door and found Inspector Walker standing on the step.

"Matt! Come in," Stanwick exclaimed, stepping aside. "It's nice of you to drop by on your way back to Royston."

Walker looked surprised.

"How did you know which direction I came from?" he asked. "I parked in the driveway, not on the street."

"Quite so, but I observe that the small mud patch by the driveway entrance on the side toward

Royston is undisturbed. Had you come from Royston, you could hardly have avoided at least grazing it as you turned in."

Walker laughed as they settled themselves into a pair of comfortable armchairs in the living room.

"Never expect to keep secrets when you visit a logician," he said. "I'm on my way back from Richford, where I've been following up some leads on the Edmunds murder last week."

"Edmunds? Isn't he the con man who was shot in a shipping warehouse?" asked Stanwick as he relit his pipe.

"That's right. We've arrested four members of a gang he recently fleeced: Cannon, Cochran, Carruthers, and Carpenter. We know one of them is the killer. Our polygraph showed that each made one true statement and one false statement this morning under interrogation, but we couldn't determine which was which."

Stanwick leaned forward eagerly. "Do you have a copy of the statements?"

Walker smiled, reached into his coat pocket, and pulled out a folded document.

"I thought you might find them interesting," he said as he handed the paper across. "If you can make any use of them, I'd be glad to hear your conclusions."

Stanwick unfolded the paper, leaned back, and read:

Cannon: I did not kill Edmunds. Carpenter is the killer.

Cochran: I did not kill Edmunds. Cannon is lying when he says Carpenter is the killer.

Carruthers: I did not kill Edmunds. Either Cannon is the killer or none of us is.

Carpenter: I did not kill Edmunds. If Carruthers did not kill Edmunds, then Cannon did.

"At least they were all consistent with their denials," Stanwick said with a laugh.

"However, a little deduction is enough to clear up the matter. The killer is..."

Q. Who is the killer?

A. pg. 208

MURDER LAKE

Jim Sukach

Dr. J.L. Quicksolve had no sooner cast out his lure when something hit his line that almost pulled the fishing rod from his hands. Suddenly he heard "Bam! Bam! Bam! Bam! Bam!"

"Sounded like gunshots," said his friend Fred Fraudstop.

Dr. Quicksolve felt his line go slack as his fish got away. "Yes, it did," he said, looking at the lake around him from the little cove where they were anchored deep in the lily pads. "Let's check it out."

They rounded a little projection of land that jutted out near their fishing spot. Now they could see more of the lake. A man was standing in a boat at a

dock behind a huge house. The house was sur-
rounded by flowers and colorful shade trees. Long,
wide concrete stairs led from the house down to the
dock. As they came closer, they saw what looked like
a body slumped over the backseat of the motorboat
the man was standing in.

Dr. Quicksolve identified himself, and the
police arrived quickly. John Joyboat said he had
been out for a
ride with his
uncle in his
motorboat.
They were just
coming back
into the dock
when a man
on the dock
shot his uncle. "He had a nine-millimeter automatic," Joyboat said. "He shot once from the dock.
Then he took a couple steps back to the stairs there
and shot several more times before he ran away past
the house."

"How do you know it was a nine-millimeter automatic?" Dr. Quicksolve asked him.

"I have one. I mean I had one like it. It was stolen about a month ago," Mr. Joyboat said.

Dr. Quicksolve walked slowly back and forth across the dock and the stairs, looking down intently. "Arrest him, officer," he said. "You had better search him and the boat. You might have to call for divers."

 What was Dr. Quicksolve talking about?

 pg. 209

SMITH & SMITH, EX-PARTNERS

Jim Sukach

There were two partners in the law firm of Smith and Smith. They were not brothers. One of them was dead. His body was found in his partner's house by his partner. Dr. J.L. Quicksolve was having lunch with his friend Sergeant Rebekah Shurshot discussing a case when she got the call on her portable receiver. They were at Mr. Smith's house in a matter of minutes, in spite of the traffic and rainy weather.

They hurried up to the door and

were let in out of the rain by one of two officers who had gotten there just ahead of them. Mr. Smith was sitting at the kitchen table. The body of the other Mr. Smith lay covered nearby.

The back door that led to the backyard had obviously been jimmied with a knife. There was water on the floor, probably tracked in by the killer. Mr. Smith was explaining, "My partner, John, was here to meet me to talk over business. We had planned to meet here, and I left the front door unlocked in case he got here first. Apparently he did, and he was sitting here when someone broke in through the back door and stabbed him. I parked my car in the garage and came in through the side door there from the garage. The killer probably heard me coming and went out this back door when he heard me drive

into the garage. I'm glad I didn't walk in on a killer with a knife!"

"Well," said Dr. Quicksolve, looking under the table.

Q. Why was he looking under the table?

A. pg. 209

PUZZLE NO.4

As Holmes and Watson sat at the dinner table waiting for Mrs. Hudson to serve another of her famous concoctions, Holmes produced a pack of playing cards. He selected five cards and placed them, face down, in a straight line in front of Watson.

"Right, Watson," said Holmes finally. "In front of you are five cards. They are made up of two diamonds, one heart, one spade and one club. Of these, two are Queens, while the other three are made up of a King, a Knave and an Ace. Match up the cards and tell me where they lie in the line up!"

"Pardon?" said Watson as he sat there with a blank expression on his face.

Holmes explained it all again, then provided Watson with the following clues:

1. Two cards separate the two Queens. 2. There are no two red cards together. 3. The third card is a King. 4. The Knave has a heart to its left and a King to its right. 5. One of the Queens is a spade.

Can you provide the answers?

 A. pg.237

COOL MICKEY

Jim Sukach

Dr. J.L. Quicksolve was packing his things on his last day in Beverly Hills. He was anxious to return to his family.

"A young woman, Betty Finn, who had a life insurance policy from us, has died," Fred Fraudstop explained to Dr. Quicksolve. "It looks like she may have been murdered by her best friend right in her own apartment."

"Did she have a fight with this friend?" Dr. Quicksolve asked.

"The police say they can't find any evidence of a fight or any motive. That's what puzzles them," Fred responded.

"Whose name was on the policy as beneficiary?"

"Her husband, of course, but he was out of the apartment when it happened."

Quicksolve asked, "How was she killed?"

"Poison," was the response.

"Let's go talk to this friend," Dr. Quicksolve said, getting up from his chair.

They arrived at the home of Mary Scapegoat, the accused friend. She was home on bail, and she came to the door.

Mr. Fraudstop introduced himself and Dr. Quicksolve. Then he asked if they could ask her a few questions. She was obviously upset about what had happened, but she said yes, she would be glad to answer questions. She let them in and began talking.

"I don't know how she was poisoned. I just know that I didn't do it," Mary Scapegoat told them.

"Tell me just what happened," Dr. Quicksolve said.

"Betty, her husband Mickey, and I were at their house. Mickey went to the kitchen to make drinks for us. When he brought the drinks out, he took a little sip of Betty's drink just before he gave it to her.

She complained and said he gave her too much ice to begin with and then he had the nerve to drink some of hers. He laughed and said he was going to get some beer. Then he left. He'd been gone about ten or fifteen minutes when Betty collapsed and fell  to the floor. I couldn't wake her, so I called an ambulance. Mickey got home just as the ambulance pulled away. I think he poisoned her, but I can't prove it, especially since I said I saw him drink from her glass. I was the last one with her, so I was arrested. I didn't do it, and I'm willing to take a lie detector test!"

"I think you'll probably pass that lie detector test, too, but I'm not so sure about Mickey. I can think of one way he might have done it," said Dr. Quicksolve.

 How?

 pg. 209

RANSOM RESCUE

Jim Sukach

Dolores Dollars had been kidnapped. A ransom note had been sent to her father demanding that two hundred thousand dollars be brought to an abandoned cabin in a remote forest area. The money was delivered, and the police had cautiously closed in from all sides. Dolores was found in the cabin blindfolded and tied up. but unharmed. She said she had been attacked from behind and kept blindfolded. She had not seen her attacker.

The police had picked up two men immediately who had been found in the area. They were sure that one was the kidnapper. They called in Dr. J.L. Quicksolve to help.

"So you have two suspects, John Dill and Frank Sweet," said Dr. Quicksolve.

"That's right," said Officer Kautchya.

"What are their alibis?"

"John claims he was out hunting and never saw the girl or anyone else. He says he's innocent, and he wants to be put in a lineup right away so he can prove it and go home. Frank says that he was just hiking in the mountains. He says he saw a few cars, but he didn't pay much attention to them. He claims he didn't kidnap the girl, and he's anxious to take a lie-detector test to prove it," said the officer.

"Get Frank's address and let him go home, but I think you'd better keep John," said Dr. Quicksolve.

Q. Why John?

A. pg. 209

COUNT THE CLUES

Jim Sukach

As Dr. J.L. Quicksolve walked toward the bank, he watched a car pull over to the curb in front of it. The driver got out of the car. Without locking the door, he looked around left and right as he approached the bank. He wore a brown jacket over a blue shirt that was not tucked in and that stuck out past the bottom of the jacket. He held his right hand in the pocket of his baggy slacks, and his left hand held a small piece of paper. He wore a green baseball cap, and he lowered his head as he walked through the door of the bank.

Quicksolve entered the bank and watched the man who had come in before him as he waited for a

teller. He saw the teller's startled expression, and when she handed the man a large bag, Dr. Quicksolve signaled the guard, whom he knew, and he took out his pistol.

When the man turned away from the teller, he was facing two guns. The guard's gun was pointed at his face, and Dr. Quicksolve's was aimed at his heart. He dropped the bag of money, and he slowly took the gun out of his pocket with two fingers and laid it on the floor.

Q. What clues gave him away to Dr. Quicksolve?
A. pg. 210

THE CASE OF THE EDGEMORE STREET SHOOTING

Stan Smith

"Thanks for coming over," Tom, said Inspector Matt Walker as Thomas P. Stanwick, the amateur logician, strolled into the inspector's office at Royston Police headquarters.

"Glad to," Stanwick replied as he flopped into a chair. "You said you were going to interrogate a suspect in that recent street shooting."

"That's right." Walker lit a cheap cigar. "As you may already know, Bruce Walder, a local business-man in his mid-fifties, was walking along Edgemore Street about dusk two days ago. Someone approached him, shot him in the chest, and ran off. We suspect that the shooter wanted to rob him, and shot him when Walder started to resist.

"We haven't located anyone who actually saw the crime, but several locals were able to describe a man they saw lounging in the street shortly before it took place. Their descriptions matched that of Victor Kravitz, a small time mugger known to frequent the area. We picked up Kravitz just a few hours ago. Let's hear what he has to say."

They went to a nearby interrogation room. Kravitz, a small, nervous man with thinning blond hair, sat beside his lawyer and chain-smoked. Two detectives leaned against the wall while Walker and Stanwick sat down at the table.

"You've got it all wrong," cried Kravitz. "I didn't shoot Walder. I was on the street earlier, sure, but just hanging around. When I saw some guy come out of an alley, come up behind the stiff, and shoot him, I ran. I didn't want no trouble."

"You saw the crime committed?" asked Walker.

"Yeah. Yeah."

"Why didn't you report it?" asked one of the other detectives.

Kravitz laughed nervously. "Sure. Like you guys were about to believe me."

"Can you describe the man?" Walker inquired.

"Sure, sure. Middle-aged guy, tall, red mustache. Wore a big gray overcoat and a hat. Walder never even saw him."

"Where did you run to?"

"My girlfriend's place. You can ask her."

Stanwick, who had been slouching back in his chair, cleared his throat and slowly sat up.

I for one have heard enough, Matt," he said to Walker. This man is obviously lying."

Q. How does Stanwick know that Kravitz is lying?

A. pg. 211

A QUIET MORNING
AT THE OFFICE

Stan Smith

"There can be no question of suicide," stated Cooper emphatically. "The murder weapon, a handgun with a silencer, was found immediately in front of the victim's desk, but beyond where he could have dropped it. It also had no fingerprints, and he wasn't wearing gloves."

"I agree," said Walker. "The gun, of course, was photographed and taken for evidence before we removed the body."

Inspector Matthew Walker of the Royston Police Department, Thomas P Stanwick, and FBI Special Agent Ryan Cooper were in the inner office of Wilson Jasper. Until he had been found shot at his desk a few hours earlier, Jasper had been a vice president of Supertech Corporation.

The reliable Sergeant Hatch entered the office and reported to Walker.

"As you can see, sir," he said, "there are only four doors out of this office. Three lead to the  offices of Jasper's aides: Joseph Springer, John King, and William Farrar. Their offices also open onto the outer hallway. The fourth door, directly facing the desk, leads to the outer office, which is occupied by Ms. Pringle, Jasper's secretary, and two clerks. The windows behind Jasper's desk cannot be opened."

While listening to Hatch's report, Stanwick glanced again over the large, bloodstained desk. When he and Walker had arrived, the body had still been slumped over the blotter, which was covered with several spattered piles of financial reports, performance evaluations, and other papers. Also on the desk were a telephone console, a pen set, a calendar, a family photograph, and a few knickknacks. A personal computer rested on a side table beside the chair.

"I've finished questioning the aides," Hatch continued. "Springer said he didn't see Jasper this morning. Jasper didn't send for him, and Springer said he didn't want to disturb him while he was doing evaluations. King and Farrar also denied seeing him this morning. Neither was sent for, and Farrar was busy with quarterly reports."

"How about Ms. Pringle?" asked Walker.

"She says Jasper arrived about eight, went right into his office, and closed the door. He had a full briefcase with him, as usual. He cleaned off his desk each night and brought a caseful of papers home."

"Did he have any appointments this morning?" asked Cooper.

"None that she knew of, and no one appeared for one. He kept his schedule and to-do list to himself. In a nutshell, no one saw anyone enter or leave Jasper's office except Jasper himself, and no one heard a shot or a noise. Ms. Pringle found the body when he wouldn't answer his intercom for a call."

"Well," said Cooper with a sigh, "a Bureau team will soon be here to examine the offices more thoroughly. It may tie in with one of our current investigations. Certainly we have established that access to the inner office was exceedingly limited."

"I think we have established rather more than that," Stanwick remarked.

"Such as?"

"Such as the identity of the killer," said Stanwick quietly.

Q. Who murdered Wilson Jasper?

A. pg. 211

PUZZLE NO.5

"Now there's a strange coincidence," said Holmes, dabbing his mouth with his napkin.

"What's that?" asked Watson.

"Each of the three tables around us has seven wine bottles placed upon it."

"How interesting," grunted Watson, returning to his meal.

"You're missing the point, Watson. I've observed that seven bottles are full, seven are half full and seven are empty.

Yet all three tables have exactly the same amount of wine upon them!"

Watson studied the surrounding three tables. "Great Scot, you're right, Holmes!" he exclaimed at last.

Can you work out the placement of the bottles? (There are two possible answers.)

A. pg.238

CRYPTIC CASES

THE STOCKBROKER'S LAST MORNING

Stan Smith

Shortly after nine one morning, Inspector Walker's car pulled up in front of a large office building in downtown Royston. With Walker was Thomas P. Stanwick, the amateur logician. Stanwick had been visiting Walker at headquarters when the call reporting the sudden death of Charles Steinberg had come in.

Stanwick and Walker hurried to Steinberg's seventh-floor office suite, from which he had run a prosperous stock brokerage firm. Passing through the carpeted reception area, they entered Steinberg's spacious office.

Steinberg's body was slumped in an easy chair

near a small, circular table in the center of the room. His tie and collar were loose. He had been dead for less than an hour, and showed no sign of bleeding. On a small table by the wall, a typewriter contained a typed note, which Stanwick read aloud.

I see no further purpose to my life and have therefore decided to end it.
I hope my family, friends, and associates will not blame themselves.
Goodbye.

Walker turned to the man in his early 30's who was standing near the office door. Jon Golding was a vice president of the firm.

"What can you tell us, Mr. Golding?"

Golding coughed nervously.

"I entered Mr. Steinberg's office earlier this morning to see him on urgent business. He was sitting in the easy chair with a cup of coffee in his hand. As soon as he saw me, he hastily drank it down. The cup had no sooner left his lips than he was seized with terrible convulsions. A few seconds later he was dead. I was horrified and ran out to the receptionist's desk, where I phoned for help. No one was allowed into the office until you arrived."

"Did you see the note in the typewriter?"

"No, sir, I did not."

"Thank you." Walker went over to Steinberg's body and searched his pockets. In the right jacket pocket he found a small glass vial, which he sniffed. "This probably contained the poison."

Stanwick sniffed it and, taking out his hand-kerchief, picked up the emptied coffee cup from

its saucer on the table and sniffed it also.

"I can detect a whiff of it here, too," he said.

Stanwick put down the coffee cup and faced Golding.

"Mr. Golding," he asked, "did Mr. Steinberg usually have his coffee in that chair?"

"Yes, sir, he drank his coffee and read the paper in that chair every morning about this time."

Stanwick pointed to a newspaper folded neatly on the table. "Did you put that there?"

Golding flushed slightly. "It was there when I came in. He wasn't reading it."

Stanwick abruptly left the office and walked to the desk of the young receptionist.

"What can you tell us, Miss Gwynne?"

"Why, little enough, I'm afraid. I heard some typing in Mr. Steinberg's office, and then Mr. Golding came out of his own office to pick up some documents for Mr. Steinberg. He went into Mr. Steinberg's office and a few moments later came rushing wildly out here and phoned for help."

"What documents did he want to show Mr. Steinberg?"

"Why, some draft pages of our weekly newsletter. He dropped them on the floor as he came back out."

Reentering Steinberg's office, Stanwick put another question to Golding. "I see there is a door between your office and this. Why didn't you use that when you came in to see him?"

"Miss Gwynne, our receptionist, had the newsletter pages I wanted to show him," Golding answered.

Stanwick quietly drew Walker aside.

"Golding is lying, Matt," he said. "This isn't suicide, but murder!"

 Q. How does Stanwick know Golding is lying?

A. pg. 212

A NEW YEAR'S DISSOLUTION

Stan Smith

Thomas P. Stanwick was still fighting off sleep as he mounted the front steps of the Dunhope home in Royston. Some way to begin a new year, he thought. After attending a New Year's Eve party, the amateur logician had been roused at six by a phone call from Inspector Walker. Robert Dunhope of Dunhope & Henson, a prosperous insurance agency, had been poisoned at a New Year's Eve party in his home, and Walker had asked Stanwick to have a look.

"Happy New Year, Tom," said Walker dourly at the door. "This way."

Walker led Stanwick into a large, well-furnished

 livingroom. Three men and a woman, still in evening clothes, sat numbly on a long sofa.

"The body has been removed," said Walker. "Mrs. Dunhope has gone down to headquarters."

"These four, I take it, were the guests at the party?" said Stanwick.

"That's right. John Merldale is—was—Dunhope's accountant. Harriet Schultze is a friend of Mrs. Dunhope and has written several popular cookbooks. Simon Henson is the junior partner in Dunhope's firm, and George Dunhope is the victim's nephew."

Stanwick sat down in an armchair across from the sofa and glanced quickly around the room. Walker took out his official notebook.

I'd like to ask the four of you to repeat to Mr.

Stanwick what you remember about the events of last night," said the inspector.

Henson, a haggard man with a trim, dark beard, gave a long sigh.

"Up until midnight," he said, "it was pretty much the same party we have together every New Year's Eve, except for George being with us."

"I'm starting my graduate studies at Royston State next week," said George.

"I've been staying with Aunt Grace and Uncle Bob until I can find a place of my own in the city."

"What went on until midnight?" asked Stanwick.

"Oh, you know," said Miss Schultze, "punch, eggnog, conversation. Bob and John started a game of chess. Shortly before midnight, Simon and I passed out some hors d'oeuvres I had prepared." She clenched a crumpled cocktail napkin and brushed away a tear.

Stanwick began toying with the tip of his mustache.

"And what happened at midnight?" he asked.

"As the hour approached," said Meridale, "we all stood up, and I filled everyone's glass with Champagne. When midnight struck, we all cheered 'Happy New Year' and drank a toast. In doing so, Simon accidentally bumped into Bob and caused him to spill some of his Champagne, but it was quickly cleaned up.

"A few moments later, though, Bob just collapsed. We thought it was a heart attack and called an ambulance. By the time the medics arrived, Bob was already dead. They checked him, said it looked suspicious, and called in the police."

"Thank you. Excuse us a moment." Stanwick stood up and stopped into the hallway with Walker. "What has the medical examiner found, Matt?"

Walker grimaced and scratched the back of his neck.

"Doc Pillsbury says it looks like a fast-acting poison. We've tested the Champagne remaining in Dunhope's glass and stained on his clothing, though, and there's no trace of poison."

"How about the hors d'oeuvres?"

"The guests say he ate only half of one. The half he didn't eat checked out clean. He didn't eat or drink anything else."

"Any food or strange objects in his pockets?"

"No, just keys, change, and a comb. That's what has us stumped, Tom. He must have been poisoned right around midnight, but we can't even figure out how he ingested the stuff."

Stanwick gave a gaping yawn before replying.

"Excuse me," he said. "If Pillsbury's results are confirmed, and no more significant facts come to light, I think I can point out the method of murder and the likely murderer."

Q. Who murdered Dunhope, and how?
A. pg. 213

THE FINAL FORECLOSURE

Derrick Niederman

It was a situation that had trouble written all over it. Niles Bronson was involved in the Ocean Towers condominium in every conceivable way: He had lived there since 1992, when the building was first constructed; he managed the condo fund, which covered all the routine expenses shared by the building's inhabitants; finally, he worked at Marine Bank, which held the mortgages on many of the condominium properties.

Several of Niles's colleagues on the condo board felt that he had conflicts of interest on the various matters that came before them. Others felt that he simply held too much influence, period. So when he was found dead in his living room one late-March evening in 1996, everyone figured it was an inside job.

No murder weapon was ever recovered, despite an immediate and exhaustive search of the entire condominium complex. But the suspicion of an "inside job" was only amplified when a search of the documents in Bronson's files revealed that three of the building's residents were facing foreclosure proceedings. That group consisted of Herman Gertner (like Bronson, a resident of Ocean Towers since its inception), real estate developer Graham Moss, and Jeff Carrington, who at one time had been a thriving restaurateur.

Each of the three men faced his own special type of financial distress. Carrington had been tracked down by his ex-wife and now faced substantial child support payments. Moss had leveraged himself to the hilt constructing an office building that was proving to be a dismal failure. And Gertner was withholding his mortgage payments until certain long-promised improvements were made to his property. Although the three men's predicaments were entirely different, what they had in common was that each had failed to meet his mortgage payments for several months. And that fact alone placed them under great scrutiny following the murder.

Actually, whoever killed Niles Bronson was lucky not to have been unmasked right away. A Mrs. Rose Kravitz, who lived in Suite 1507, just around the corner from Bronson's Suite 1516, claimed that she had passed a strange man in the hallway as she took out the garbage late that afternoon. Ocean Towers was a fairly small, close-knit community; those on any particular floor tended to recognize those from the same floor, and this man simply didn't belong. At the time, though, Rose didn't think much about the stranger, nor did she get a good look at him. All she remembered was that he was wearing a T-shirt and some cut-off blue jeans.

That same evening, Rose had some business to discuss with Niles Bronson, and she was perplexed when he didn't answer her knock. Hadn't he said he would be in? She said that she had made sure to knock at halftime of the NCAA semifinal game between UMass and Kentucky, in order not to catch him at a bad time. She could hear the TV from outside, though, and became suspicious when her repeated knocks brought nothing. She waited until the game was over, at which point she renewed her efforts and finally called building superintendent, Win Scheinblum. Scheinblum opened the door to find Bronson's body on the floor, not far from his TV set. "Tales from the Crypt" was blaring in the background. It was evident that Bronson had been stabbed, but there was no sign of any weapon. It was only then that Rose Kravitz remembered the strange man and wondered whether he might have been involved.

However, just two nights after Bronson's murder, mayhem turned to madness in the form of another tragedy at Ocean Towers. None other than Herman Gertner was found lying on the busy walkway in front of the building, having apparently fallen from his balcony. He was alive, but just barely. He remained unconscious, unable to shed any light on what had happened to him, and hopes for his recovery were dim indeed.

As you might expect, when all else failed, Inspector Forsooth was called in to investigate. Forsooth went first to Herman Gertner's condo. He found the door to the outside balcony still open. The balcony had a three-foot-high protective metal railing, but several of its screws had come loose, and it wasn't sturdy enough to prevent the tragedy. Next came the Bronson murder scene. Nothing had been touched since the murder, except that the TV had been turned off and, of course, the body had been removed. A search for fingerprints had come up empty. Forsooth then proceeded to Graham Moss's apartment. Surprisingly, Moss was nothing short of ecstatic. He had just lined up a large accounting firm to lease several floors of his faltering office building, and he relished the thought that his financial problems might be solved after all.

When Forsooth then spoke to the security personnel at the front desk, they confirmed that all three men on the "foreclosure list" had been on the premises for most of the day of Bronson's murder. Jeff Carrington had been out that morning, but he returned at about 2:00 P.M. and they didn't see him afterwards. They did see Graham Moss, who left at about 7:00 P.M. for a dinner engagement. And Herman Gertner left at about 8:00 P.M. to go bowling.

Forsooth's final stop was to interview Jeff Carrington, whose apartment was the most splendid of them all. Carrington admitted that he had gotten caught up in a free-wheeling, free-spending lifestyle, but it was now time to reform. He was trying to work out suitable arrangements to pay child support on time, but he conceded that staying at Ocean Towers was probably out of the question. He did ask how Herman Gertner was doing, and it was Inspector Forsooth's sad duty to inform him that Gertner had not survived his fall.

On his way out, Forsooth ran into none other than Rose Kravitz, who admitted that some morbid fascination had made her decide to go out and gawk at the mark in the pavement where Gertner had landed. She also admitted that she wondered whether he might have been the man she saw on Saturday, right about the time that Niles Bronson was killed.

But Forsooth didn't think so. In fact, it didn't take long for him to realize that there had been a conspiracy to kill Niles Bronson—one that involved two of our three suspects. And he knew precisely how they worked together. Do you?

1) Who killed Niles Bronson?
2) What was the role of the accomplice?
3) Who killed Herman Gertner and why?

INSPECTOR FORSOOTH ANSWERS YOUR QUESTIONS

Q1. What do we know about the motive for Bronson's murder?

We have to assume that considerable ill will had built up between Bronson and one of the men being foreclosed.

Q2. Does what the man in the hallway was wearing mean anything?

Actually, it does. His attire suggests that he wasn't hiding anything on his person.

Q3. Why were the killers "lucky not to have been unmasked right away"?

All that meant is that if Rose Kravitz had gotten a better look, she might have been able to positively ID him.

Q4. Did "Tales from the Crypt" come on directly after the game, that is, on the same channel?

No, it did not. "Tales from the Crypt" was on FOX, whereas the NCAA games were on CBS.

Q5. What was the time of the fatal attack on Bronson?

Well, my previous answer actually gives something of a clue. Remember, Bronson was a big basketball fan and wouldn't have missed those games for the world.

Q6. What floor did Gertner live on?

I'm not sure of the exact floor, but there's an

important inference available here, one that's quite relevant to the solution.

Q7. What kinds of repair needed to be done to Gertner's condo?

Wouldn't you know it? His balcony needed repairing. Gertner felt that it was dangerous, and it looks as though he was right.

Q8. When do they fire up the incinerator?

Well, in this day and age, Ocean Towers didn't have an incinerator. But trash disposal is a vital ingredient to this crime, that's for sure!

Q9. Why wasn't the work done on Gertner's condo?

He always felt it was because he wasn't as wealthy as some of the other occupants of the building, and therefore didn't carry as much clout.

Q10. Did it matter that Carrington's condo was the most splendid of all of them?

Actually, in a curious way, that fact is a nice little clue, once you think about the various factors that can make an oceanfront condo splendid.

Q11. Is there an exit to the building that doesn't go by the security personnel?

No, there isn't.

Q12. Was the murder weapon dropped down an incinerator shaft?

Great question! The incinerator part has already been covered, but the shaft is a great place to look. Remember, though, the garbage area in the basement was thoroughly inspected, and they didn't come up with a murder weapon.

 Can you solve the mystery?

A. pg. 214

PUZZLE NO.6

Sherlock Holmes had received two telegrams from the infamous Professor Moriarty within a space of 3 hours. The first was a threat against the famous detective's life, while the second said that he, the professor, had organized a present for Holmes. The remainder of the second telegram contained the following riddle:

He who makes it, makes it to sell. He who buys it, does not use it.

He who uses it, does not know it.

Watson read both telegrams. "It doesn't make sense to me, Holmes," said Watson. "First he threatens your life and then he organizes a present for you."

"Solve the riddle, Watson. Then you'll see that it makes sense," replied Holmes.

What was it that Moriarty intended to send Holmes?

A. pg.238

DEATH AT THE CLINIC

Stan Smith

"It's your bad luck, old chum," said Thomas P. Stanwick, the amateur logician, "that I recently made a special study of the Queen's Gambit Declined. That's when I found that innovation against your Cambridge Springs Defense that helped me win tonight."

Inspector Matthew Walker grunted. "Unfortunately, a working cop doesn't have time to keep up with your theoretical novelties. Good game, though."

Stanwick and Walker were relaxing in armchairs in the lounge of the Royston Chess Club following their weekly game. The windows were open to the warm evening air.

"How are Elizabeth and the boys?" asked Stanwick as he lit his pipe.

"Just fine, thanks," replied Walker. "When I left, Elizabeth was on the phone with one of her friends talking about their awful soap opera."

"'Awful soap opera' is not a very exclusive term. Which one?"

"'All My Nights.' An hour of guff. It's also popular, I've learned, in one of the best nutrition clinics in the city."

"Indeed?" Stanwick smiled and arched his eyebrows. "And how would a well-fed fellow like you know that?"

"A murder case. Dr. Mila Dixon runs a private clinic on the East End, and one of her nutritionists, Lola Alvarez, was shot to death last Wednesday."

"I see." Stanwick's face relaxed into pensiveness. "Any suspects? And what's the connection with 'All My Nights'?"

"We have three suspects, all regular clients of

Lola's. Malcolm Beard, a neurosurgeon, arrived just as 'All My Nights', which begins at 1:30, was ending. He went in to Lola's consulting room and hurried out, looking pale. One of the other nutritionists, Ellen Tiffany, shopped at Rosella's, a downtown boutique, for two hours after it opened and arrived back at the clinic half an hour later. Her arrival coincided with that of Frank McGowan, a building contractor. He was there exactly as long after the noon factory whistle four blocks away sounded as he was there before it."

"When does Rosella's open?"

"Nine."

"And the third suspect?"

"A personal-injury lawyer named Arthur Workman. Our witnesses have him arriving 45 minutes after McGowan left. He stayed half an hour to an hour."

Stanwick idly twisted the tip of his brown mustache.

"Interesting," he said. "Who discovered the body?"

"Mila, at about three. A silencer had been used on the gun. Lola was lying beside a tall scale. Beneath her was a smashed clock showing 1:44, which Doc Pillsbury says is consistent with the medical evidence as the time of death. The killer wasn't necessarily the last one to arrive, since any of them might have been too scared to report the body."

"Have you made the arrest yet?"

Walker shook his head. "We're still investigating."

"Fair enough." Stanwick tapped some ashes out of his pipe. "Assuming that the killer is one of your three suspects, however, a little deduction reveals which one it is."

Q. Who murdered Lola Alvarez?

 pg. 216

DEATH COMES TO THE COLONEL

Stan Smith

Thomas P. Stanwick, the amateur logician, and Inspector Matthew Walker of the Royston Police strode into the richly carpeted study of Jeremy Huddleston. It was a chilly Tuesday in late fall, and Stanwick had heen chatting in Walker's offlce when word came in of Huddleston's sudden death. Poisoning was suspected.

Huddleston, a retired army colonel in his seventies, lay behind his desk in the middle of the room, partly covered by his overturned chair. His sightless eyes stared at the ceiling as a fire crackled in the large brick hearth behind the desk. Near the hearth, a young, balding man sat wearily in an armchair.

Walker approached him.

"Mr. Huddleston?" he asked. "Mr. George Huddleston?"

The young man nodded.

"The colonel's grand-nephew, aren't you?"

"Yes."

"Please tell us what happened."

Huddleston looked up nervously and wet his lips. "I came into the study about ten this morning to say good morning to Uncle Jeremy. He was working at his desk and seemed to be in cheerful spirits. He asked me to pour him another cup of coffee from the sideboard, so I did. He drank about half of it, and then suddenly put his cup down and said, 'Before I forget, I must call Phillips to fix the leak in the basement pipes.'"

"Roy Phillips, the local plumber?" Walker cut in.

"That's right." Huddleston continued. "He had just started to dial his private phone when he uttered a sharp cry, clutched suddenly at his throat, and fell over onto the floor. I was horrified and rushed over to him, but could see at once that he was dead.

"Hurrying out to the hall, I locked the study door and called to his housekeeper, Mrs. Stowe, who phoned the doctor and the police. I kept the study door locked until you arrived."

A medical assistant touched Walker on the shoulder.

"Excuse me, sir," he said. "The drops we extracted from the coffee cup show definite traces of cyanide."

Walker nodded. Stanwick lit his pipe and looked slowly around the room. His gaze rested in turn on the cheery fire warming the room of death, on the half-empty coffee cup resting neatly in its saucer, and on the West Point ring adorning the victim's finger.

"Do you live here, Mr. Huddleston?" Stanwick asked, suddenly turning to the nephew.

"No," replied Huddleston. "I live in California, where I work for an architectural firm. I was here only for the week, to visit Uncle Jeremy and see the East Coast again."

The phone on the colonel's desk rang. Walker answered it and bluntly told the caller, an old friend of the colonel's nephew, that the colonel was dead and a police investigation was in progress. After hanging up, he faced George Huddleston again.

"What more can you tell us, Mr. Huddleston?" he asked.

"Nothing," replied Huddleston listlessly.

"On the contrary," said Stanwick sharply, "I think Mr. Huddleston could help by telling us the truth."

Q. How does Stanwick know that Huddleston is lying?

A. pg. 217

THE PIANO REQUITAL

Derrick Niederman

As Gilbert von Stade performed, there wasn't an aficionado in the house who didn't marvel at his mastery of the keyboard. Von Stade was playing Chopin's Etude in G-flat, Opus 10, No. 5, a most challenging piece by anyone's standards, even for a world-class pianist such as von Stade. The piece wasn't particularly long, as a number of performers were being showcased that night in a concert to benefit the city's sagging Foundation for the Arts. Yet it was a spellbinding few minutes.

When his work was done, von Stade got up from the piano to acknowledge a raucous standing ovation, which had become the norm at his performances. He was loved by virtually all who followed the music world; whereas other musicians of his talent tended to be aloof, he was known for being gracious and generous with his time. He took delight in the crowd, and always mingled after his concerts. But there was to be no mingling on this particular night. Against the backdrop of the applause, von Stade suddenly froze up and fell to the stage. The curtain was closed and the show came to a temporary halt. Gilbert von Slade would never regain consciousness.

At first, no one suspected foul play. Gilbert von Stade was a fairly old man, after all, and most everyone in the audience assumed that he had suffered a heart attack. Yet the autopsy would later reveal that his death was anything but natural. Traces of the rare but deadly batrachotoxin were found in his system, and had surely been responsible for his death. It was murder, all right, but it remained to determine just who could have committed such a dastardly deed.

It turned out (surprise, surprise) that there was

more to the decedent's true character than was ever seen by his adoring public. As is all too often the case within the highest echelon of musical talent, von Stade was an extremely demanding person to work with, and his own search for perfection often victimized those around him. Many thought him hypocritical for basking in the public glory of his music in the wake of exhausting practice sessions in which he had bullied and badgered everyone in sight.

Perhaps because of von Stade's pre-eminence, there was considerable friction within the group of musicians performing that night. Two younger pianists, Heinrich Albertson and Vivien Frechette, were also on the evening program, and were extremely eager to prove themselves. Albertson had come on before von Stade, and had given an absolutely flawless rendition of another Chopin etude: C-Major, Opus 10, No. 1. Frechette, on the other hand, was scheduled to play immediately following von Stade, but her performance was delayed by the onstage tragedy. In fact, some of those backstage had qualms about continuing the concert under the circumstances. Stage manager Sophia Brightwell, a frequent target of von Stade's tirades, tried to convince Frechette that it would be inappropriate for her to play, but Frechette would have nothing of it. She reminded everyone that von Stade was a professional, and always lived up to the standard that the show must go on.

No one doubted that with von Stade out of the way, Albertson and Frechette had a better chance of success in their own musical careers. However, they certainly weren't the only suspects in the murder, for the rivalry had extended to the people in all of their lives, even if these very people had made a special effort that evening to heal all past wounds.

Marla Albertson, Beatrice von Stade, and Samuel Frechette never completely took to their positions as musicians' spouses. They were still very much in love with their respective mates, but they weren't necessarily attuned to their every note, so to speak. Marla Albertson was especially out of the loop, being unable to read sheet music, much less play it, but she had many other talents. One was cooking, and that night she organized a pre-concert dinner, full of special culinary treats. She prepared frog's-leg appetizers, and encouraged others to make their own contributions. Samuel Frechette brought some homemade bread and Beatrice von Stade whipped up some linguine with pesto sauce. These offerings were joined by those from many other performers and their families, as the invitees included several dozen musicians who would play that night, not just the pianists.

Although everyone applauded Marla for her initiative, the food selections weren't of universal appeal. Some of the musicians had no appetite because of pre-concert nerves, while others were reluctant to get too adventurous with their food choices while dressed in white tie. Among the pianists, only Gilbert von Stade was willing to handle greasy foods such as the frog's legs, but he made a special point of thoroughly washing his hands in the backstage men's room. On the subject of von Stade's food choices, a curious recollection of the evening's emcee, Walter Penwinkle, was that von Stade had garlic on his breath when he collapsed—on his dying breath, at that. Penwinkle and Sophia Brightwell had been the first people to rush to the stricken artist's aid, albeit in a futile cause.

After von Stade's death, the concert was delayed, but it resumed just minutes later with Vivien Frechette at the keyboard, playing Chopin's Etude in E-Flat Minor, Opus 10, No. 6. The piece was slow and melancholy, if not downright mournful, a perfect choice under the circumstances. Then, in a tribute to von Stade, Frechette astonished all the spectators by playing the precise piece von Stade had played earlier. She, too, got a rousing ovation.

Some days later, Inspector Forsooth was called in to unravel the mystery of just what happened during that ill-fated concert. He paid a visit to the stage where von Stade had fallen, and took time to survey the men's room in the back, where von Stade had washed his hands. There he found soap, toothpaste, mouthwash, some Breath-Assure tablets, and even a vial of DMSO, which Sophia Brightwell said von Stade used to take for his arthritis, before tiring of its side effects. Forsooth realized that the telling proof behind the von Stade killing might be hard to come by, but now he knew where to look.

INSPECTOR FORSOOTH ANSWERS YOUR QUESTIONS

Q1. What is batrachotoxin?

Batrachotoxin is best known as the poison used by some South American tribes to coat their hunting arrows. The poison comes from the secretions of a certain species of tree frog. The natives would dip their arrows into the frog secretions, so even if the arrows didn't cause fatal wounds, the batrachotoxin would. (Not my style, but that's life in the jungle for you.)

Q2. Did Samuel Frechette bring garlic bread to dinner?

Nice try, but no. He brought plain bread.

Q3. How could a food poison get specifically to von Stade if the non-musicians were eating some of everything?

Good question. I haven't the foggiest idea how that would be possible.

Q4. Does the linguine have garlic in it?

The linguine doesn't have any garlic in it, but the pesto sauce is loaded with it. However, there is a pretty good clue that this didn't kill von Stade.

Q5. Are the pieces played by the pianists relevant?

Yes, they are all relevant.

Q6. What were the unwanted side effects of DMSO?

Nice question. The answer is that von Stade detested the fact that DMSO left him with a gar-licky taste in his mouth! (Yes, that's an actual side effect, and it was especially intolerable for von Stade, who liked to mingle with his adoring fans.)

Q7. Does Frechette play with gloves?

No, none of them played with gloves. Another nice question, though!

Q8. Could the pianist who played before him have put the poison onto the keys?

No, that would have been extremely difficult to do, because he was in plain view of the audience the whole time. We have to assume the poison was placed there just before the show began.

Q9. What was so difficult about von Stade's piece?

Ah, I was hoping you would ask. The answer is that the piece is more difficult because it's harder for the fingers to move around on keys that are smaller!

Q10. Did everyone know what piece of music von Stade was playing that night?

Certainly all the musicians did, and everyone involved with the show did.

Q11. Could the toxin have been absorbed by the skin?

Sure could, if mixed with DMSO. One of the properties of DMSO is that it is readily absorbed through the skin, and in its liquid form is capable of carrying other compounds right along with it.

Q12. Is it possible that the victim was killed by accident, and that one of the other musicians was the actual target?

It's quite possible, and it's a great question. However, that wasn't the case, and it's our job to show how we know that.

Q. Can you solve the mystery?

A. pg. 217

PUZZLE NO.7

While working on a case Holmes received vital information from a mysterious source in the form of a note.

The note read:

> Go to the Dunwick Bank. Inside each of the safety deposit boxes listed below you will find a clue to the crime you are presently investigating.
> BOX NUMBERS: 20, 80, 76, 19, 23, 92, 88 and ?
> I have omitted to tell you the number of the last box, but I'm sure a great detective such as yourself will know where to look.

Holmes read the note, then passed it to Dr. Watson.

"Most inconvenient," muttered Watson. "Now we'll have to open every single safety deposit box to find the clue."

"Not so, Watson," replied Holmes. "I know exactly which box to open. Come along, let's hurry to the Dunwick Bank."

What was the number of the last safety deposit box?

 pg.238

MURDER AT THE CHESSBOARD

Stan Smith

Thomas P. Stanwick and Inspector Matthew Walker were seated one afternoon in Stanwick's living room, chatting about recent crime news.

"You may have seen something in the papers," said Walker, "about the murder two nights ago of Professor Richard Hansford."

"Yes, I think so." Stanwick frowned. "The archaeologist. He was stabbed in the back while seated at a chessboard in his study, wasn't he? Killed instantly."

"That's right. A call came in to headquarters at 8:30 last Wednesday night from Michael Rimbach, a visiting relative of Hansford's.

"When the squad car arrived, Rimbach explained to the officers that he had heard a cry from the study as he was passing by in the hallway. Looking in, he saw the professor slumped back in his chair and caught a glimpse of a man escaping through the French doors of the study onto the lawn. Rimbach rushed to the doors, but the man had already disappeared into the rainy darkness.

"Hansford was obviously dead, so without touching anything, Rimbach called the police and told Hansford's sister Emily of the crime. Emily, an invalid, had heard nothing.

"Rimbach thinks he recognized the man as David Kunst, a neighbor who played chess with Hansford every Wednesday evening at 7:30. They were both enthusiasts of monochromatic chess, and played no other kind."

"Really?" said Stanwick. "Chess in which no piece can move from a black square to a white square, or vice versa? That's quite rare."

"Yes, it is, which is why they played it so regularly. It's hard to find partners for it. Rimbach, the

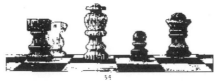

sister, and Kunst all confirmed the weekly games."

"When we interviewed Kunst at his home later that evening," Walker continued, "he said he had received a call from Rimbach a little after seven saying that Hansford was ill and had to cancel that evening's game. Kunst said he therefore spent the evening at home. Rimbach denies having called him. Kunst lives alone, and there were no witnesses. We saw a damp overcoat and shoes there, but he says they got wet on his way home from work."

"In what condition did you find the study?" Stanwick asked.

"The French doors were open. We looked for footprint traces on the lawn, but found nothing definite. The condition of the board indicated that a game was in progress when the murder occurred."

"Did the board look like the game had been in progress for an hour?"

"Yes, I guess so. It looked like the players were

entering the middle part of the game. A knight and two bishops were already posted in the center of the board."

"Had the weekly game ever been called off before?"

"Now and then. Usually the sister phoned Kunst if Hansford was ill. She had been confined to her bed that day, though, and hadn't seen her brother."

"Well," said Stanwick, fingering the tip of his mustache, "you have an interesting but thoroughly contradictory pair of stories to consider. One of them is patently untrue, however, so I suggest you concentrate your inquiry in the direction of the liar."

Q. Who is lying?

A. pg. 220

THE CHURCHILL LETTER

Stan Smith

"Mrs. Bryant! It's nice to see you again. Please come in."

Thomas P. Stanwick stood back from the door and waved his gray-haired visitor into his living room.

"I'm sorry to bother you again, Mr. Stanwick," said Ellen Bryant as she settled herself onto the sofa, "but you were so helpful with my earlier difficulty that I hoped you might advise me on this one."

"Certainly, if I can," replied Stanwick. Striding to the sideboard, he began to prepare a tray of fresh tea. "What's the problem?"

"A few days ago," she said, "I was visited by

Stephen Faybush, the nephew of a couple I know in my neighborhood. He specializes in unusual invest-ments."

"Indeed?" said Stanwick. He brought the tray over and poured two cups of Lapsang souchong. "Have you been looking for investment advice?"

"Well, I have a small nest egg that isn't earning much in the bank, and I may have mentioned this to my neighbors."

"And what sorts of investment does this Faybush promote?"

"Historical artifacts, mostly. Famous signatures and such. He says they consistently beat inflation as they rise in value over time."

"That's true—if they are genuine, that is." Stanwick settled himself near her on the sofa. "Do you by chance have such an item in your folder there?"

"Exactly, yes." Mrs. Bryant opened a manila folder she had been carrying and extracted a letter "It's a Churchill," she said as she handed it to Stanwick.

Stanwick held the document gingerly and gave a low whistle.

"A letter from Churchill's private secretary to a John McMasters," he murmured. "Not a name I recognize. Probably a constituent. 'Sir Winston very much appreciates the book you sent him' and so on. Dated in mid-1950. Cream-colored paper. Letterhead refers to Chartwell, Churchill's country home. The valuable bit is the handwritten inscription 'With warmest good wishes, Winston S. Churchill' along the bottom after the secretary's signature. Only about a year and a half later, he returned to power as Prime Minister."

"Stephen is urging me to buy it," said Mrs. Bryant. "He is letting me keep it and look it over this week."

Stanwick smiled faintly.

"My advice," he said, "is to have nothing more

to do with Mr. Faybush. In fact, I think I'll place a call to the local constabulary about him. This letter is a fraud. May I suggest that you find a good mutual fund for your money?"

 How does Stanwick know the letter is a fraud?

pg. 221

PIER FOR THE COURSE

Derrick Niederman

Inspector Forsooth's next case shows how dangerous it is to play with guns—especially when hard-core, aggressive corporate types are involved. The occasion of interest to us is the off-site meeting of the Fairport Firearms Company. For several years the firm's senior and middle managers had met at some unusual locales to bond, try out different management techniques, and ultimately to test the mettle of all those who attended. This time around, the group agreed to go on a hunting and fishing expedition at Lake Nineveh. It was a decision that permanently changed the company and the lives of those who worked for it.

The focus of the weekend was on three of the company's vice presidents, all of whom were extremely hungry for professional advancement: David Willoughby, the chief financial officer; Kevin Van Allen, the head of the sales division; and Paula Fine, the marketing director. Each of these three was the head of a corporate "team" for the off-site meeting. The reason this turned out to be important is that only the team leaders spent any time by themselves—everyone who worked under them was always in a group, with others to attest to their whereabouts. The three groups took turns occupying different areas of the lakeside, each of which offered its own special terrain. Although no hunting was done per se, everyone had real guns and blanks for use in the role-playing survival games that the teams were engaging in. The whole idea of the weekend was to create a primitive setting that would develop ingenuity and teamwork.

Tragedy struck at lunchtime on the second day of the meeting. Each employee had been given a lunch box containing a peanut-butter-and-jelly sandwich, potato chips, bottled water, and, finally, a caramel apple to celebrate the fall season. The only exception to the rule was senior vice president Wayne Metzger, the second-most-powerful person in the company; he was given a ham sandwich instead of the standby PB&J because of a longstanding and extremely serious allergy to peanut oil. Metzger and company president Bart Strunk were the only two who didn't participate in the management games that morning. Instead, they located themselves on a pier that jutted out into the lake, prepared to enjoy some relaxing trout fishing. But neither one made it off the pier alive.

The first people to reach the crime scene were David Willoughby and his assistant, Sharon Sturgis. In a sense, their appearance was surprising, because just prior to the lunch break Willoughby's group had been out at Rocky Point, the most remote locale of them all. But they wanted to see how the fishing was going—and perhaps pick up a few corporate brownie points—so they headed to the pier. They saw the bodies from a distance and ran toward them.

Sturgis tried in vain to revive Metzger, who had collapsed for unknown reasons. Willoughby went farther out on the pier, where Bart Strunk lay dead. Strunk had been shot twice in the chest. Willoughby noted to his assistant that the two must have just finished their lunch, as the core of Strunk's caramel apple lay beside him, still white. Metzger's sandwich was finished, but he hadn't gotten to his apple yet. The bottled water, plastic cups, and potato chip bags were strewn around the pier. Clearly the men hadn't had a chance to clean up.

The other two groups—led by Kevin Van Allen and Paula Fine—were quickly called in, and the fun and games stopped right there. Because the woods had been resounding with fake gunfire throughout the day, no one could be sure exactly where the shots that hit Bart Strunk had come from, or, for that matter, when they had been fired. But the murder weapon was eventually fished out of the lake, not far from the pier. Fittingly, Strunk had been shot by one of his firm's own guns.

The search for clues began, and a number of

interesting facts turned up. Some had to do with the corporate intrigue at Fairport Firearms, such as the fact that Van Allen and Fine had a romantic relationship. They had tried to keep the relationship a secret, but they were caught red-handed on Lake Nineveh: When asked what they were doing during the time just before the discovery of the bodies, they had no choice but to admit that they had sneaked away for a romantic liaison in the woods. The two seemed embarrassed by the disclosure, but they realized that it would have looked much worse if they had been unable to account for their whereabouts. In any event, many people in the company had figured out that Van Allen and Fine had long-term plans for themselves as a couple, plans that included running Fairport Firearms one day.

The odd man out among the three vice presidents was David Willoughby, who had a particularly close working relationship with the late Wayne Metzger. Metzger, as senior vice president, apparently treated Willoughby roughly, and took full use of the corporate power he held. However,

Willoughby was also fiercely loyal to Metzger, and always saw to it that Metzger's personal quirks were satisfied. He figured that if Metzger was going to be running the show at some point, it made sense to play along.

As far as the off-site meeting went, the murder investigation confirmed some basic details. First of all, because there were so many extra guns around, the murder weapon could not be pinned on any one person or team. However, it was readily determined that the group led by Paula Fine had been in the area closest to the pier for the 20 minutes or so prior to the discovery of the bodies. Sturgis added that as part of standard procedure, she had double-checked Metzger's box lunch after Willoughby's initial check and didn't notice anything wrong with it.

Inspector Forsooth surveyed the evidence and came to a surprising conclusion—that the deaths had resulted from a two-person conspiracy! More than that, there was a twist at the end, because Forsooth claimed that one of the co-conspirators had pulled a double cross! Your job is to determine who spoiled the fun and games at Lake Nineveh. Specifically, you must answer the following questions:

1) Who killed Bart Strunk?
2) Who killed Wayne Metzger?
3) How was Metzger killed? Be specific as to how the crime was perpetrated.

INSPECTOR FORSOOTH ANSWERS YOUR QUESTIONS

Q1. Did Metzger collapse because he ate something containing peanut oil?

That's right. It was determined that Metzger died from an allergic reaction that closed his larynx, and traces of peanut oil were found in his stomach.

Q2. Was Metzger poisoned by something in his lunch?

The answer, literally speaking, is no. But he was poisoned, all right. (Note that peanut oil isn't a poison as such, but it is considered a poison in this case, given Metzger's allergy.)

Q3. Did the bottled water or cups play an important role?

The answer is an emphatic yes. The existence of the cups was an essential part of the conspiracy, believe it or not.

Q4. From what distance was Strunk shot?

It simply wouldn't have been possible for anyone to have shot Strunk from afar, because the shots came from an almost head-on angle, eliminating the possibility that the killer had been farther down along the shore. And because of the dense woods, the shots would never have gotten through unless the killer was near the shore.

Q5. Does that mean that someone in the group closest to the pier must have fired the shot?

Absolutely. Remember, though, those groups rotated.

Q6. Which group was scheduled to have been closest to the pier after the lunch break?

Kevin Van Allen's.

Q7. Was it a coincidence that Sharon Sturgis attended to Wayne Metzger?

Not at all. The entire murder plot depended on who took care of which corpse!

Q8. How long does an allergy to peanut oil take to set in?

Not very long. Metzger probably didn't last more than 15 seconds or so.

Q9. Was it the candied apple that was laced with peanut oil? And did someone know that Metzger was going to eat Strunk's apple?

Believe it or not, the answer to both questions is a resounding yes!

Q10. Was one of the dead guys involved in the conspiracy?

Again, yes!

Q11. Did Willoughby have an alibi?

His alibi was that the apple was still white. Given that he was in a remote locale just prior to when the body was found, it appeared that he couldn't have been involved, because an apple core will turn brown fairly quickly if left out in the open.

Q12. Who died first, Strunk or Metzger?

Great question. The answer is that Strunk died first.

Q. Can you solve the mystery?
A. pg. 221

PUZZLE NO.8

Over a period of a few weeks a number of prominent people had been kidnapped by the evil Professor Moriarty and held for ransom.

"We must find out who his next victim will be, Watson!" exclaimed Holmes.

"But how do we do that, Holmes?" replied Watson.

Just then a note was delivered to 221b Baker Street. It was from Moriarty and on the note was written: "23406 306 will be next!"

From this Holmes was able to identify the next victim. Can you?

 pg.238

SABOTAGE AT CENTIPORE

Stan Smith

The Fourth floor of the Centipore building, which
housed   the Engineering division, seldom had
visitors. The medical membranes produced by
Centipore were designed there, so the corporate
security chief, Abraham Freedman, kept Engineering
a restricted area.

Some tampering with a sensitive computer disk,
however, had brought two visitors to the fourth
floor. Inspector Matthew Walker and Thomas P.
Stanwick were in the office of Sylvia DiCampli, the
vice-president of Engineering.

"The disk contains plans for a valuable membrane prototype, Inspector," DiCampli said. "It's kept in the storage room down the hall. The disk was fine when used last Wednesday, the 11th, but was found to be altered last Friday, the 13th. Harry Miller, the senior engineer who discovered the problem, reported it to me. I immediately confimed it and reported it to Lester Parke, the executive vice-president of operations. He called your people."

"Sergeant Hatch tells me that the door to the storage room was unforced," said Walker. "Therefore it was accessed by the swipe of a magnetic card. Please tell me who had access to that room."

"Besides myself and Harry Miller, that would be two other senior engineers, Tom Donlan and Chris Delaney, and Mr. Parke. Tom is new here, though, so for now he can get access to the room only with verification by one of the others."

"Couldn't Mr. Freedman authorize access for someone else?" asked Stanwick.

"Technically, yes," DiCampli replied, "but that would be highly irregular. Besides, he was laid up with the flu all last week, and conducted no business."

"I'd like another look at the room," said Walker, standing up.

A moment later, the three of them were in the small storage room. The walls were lined with shelves of floppy disk containers. DiCampli pointed

out the container with the altered disk, which sat on a separate side shelf. A computer terminal rested on a small table against the center wall.

"Is the altered disk usually kept on that shelf?" asked Stanwick.

"That's right," replied DiCampli.

"And it was not altered on this terminal?"

"Correct. This terminal makes a note on its hard drive whenever it is used. We have verified the normal use on the 11th and the use on the 13th, when Harry discovered the problem. The disk was not used here between those times."

"You also told my sergeant that using the disk on another computer would require a decryption code," said Walker.

"Yes, and the code was changed on the 9th. It's issued automatically to senior engineers, and is available to myself and higher ups through Freedman."

"What damage to the company, Ms. DiCampli, could have resulted from the alteration of the disk?" asked Stanwick.

"It could have been worse. The alteration was discovered just in time to prevent a false patent application and costly failures in testing. Our competitors would have loved a delay in the discovery."

A short while later, Stanwick and Walker were eating lunch in the company cafeteria.

"Industrial espionage!" remarked Stanwick. "You don't often get those cases."

"True!" replied Walker with a rueful smile. "The chief still has me working as an Inspector Without Portfolio. It keeps my work varied."

"Anything interesting that you haven't told DiCampli?"

"In fact, yes." Walker leaned forward and spoke softly. "I have strong evidence that one of Centipore's competitors—one 10 times its size—selected, approached, and bribed at least one Centipore employee. We don't know which employee, though."

"Ah!" Stanwick took a pen and a pocket pad from his shirt pocket. "In that case, if all that DiCampli has told us checks out, I believe I can jot down who is responsible for the alteration of the disk."

Q. Who altered the Centipore disk?

A. pg. 224

HALLOWEEN HORROR

Derrick Niederman

Being a ghost for Halloween is one thing. Becoming a ghost is another. But that's what happened to one teenage girl on this scariest of Halloweens.

The trick-or-treating part of the evening went about as expected, with house after house trembling as her wispy figure made its way up the front steps. The ghost lived in a town where folks took their costumes seriously, and people were especially generous to inspired creations. By the time the night was through, she had amassed enough goodies to last her until Thanksgiving. But she didn't last even one day, thanks to a fatal choice of late-night snack.

In the ghost's possession at the time of her death

was a half-eaten Butterfinger bar, which was immediately sent to the toxicology lab. The results showed that the candy bar had been laced with rat poison: It must have been doctored and rewrapped, but the ghost never noticed it. But even if the question of how she died could be resolved, it wasn't at all clear who might have wanted her out of the way.

In real life, the ghost was in junior high school. She was a good student, seemingly without an enemy in the world. She was also a shoo-in to make the cheerleading squad for the upcoming basketball season. And with that small fact, a motive began to take shape. The problem was that the candy bar could have come from virtually anybody along her Halloween route.

The ghost's route on her final Halloween journey was painstakingly retraced, and some curious facts turned up: For one, she had been trick-or-treating with a group of friends until fairly late in the evening, and all were pretty sure that the ghost hadn't picked up any Butterfinger bars during their escapades. But after leaving her friends, she had gone to four houses in a final circle near her own home. And of those four families, three of them had a daughter who was vying for the same cheerleading squad! The families in question were the Ackmans, the Bartosavages, and the Claxtons, whom the ghost visited in that order. Her final stop came at Old Lady MacDonald's house up on the hill; the old lady was a widow, and her kids had all grown up and moved away.

The interviews with these residents left the police no closer than they had been at first. Everyone professed outrage at the heinous Halloween crime that had shaken the neighborhood. Each said that the ghost was one of the last trick-or-treaters they had that night (the earlier part of the evening having been taken up with younger kids), and each of them fiercely denied an attempt to poison for the sake of cheerleading—although they had all heard stories abour such overzealous parents.

Not wanting to miss any detail, the police compiled records of how everyone was disguised that night. It turned out that Mr. Ackman had greeted his arrivals in his customary devil suit. Mrs. Bartosavage had greeted her callers in a light-up skeleton costume whose bones glowed in the dark. Mr. Claxton had devised a special outfit in which a woman's mask, etc., were placed on his back, so that he approached his guests facing backwards! When he turned around, the effect was creepy indeed. And Old Lady MacDonald, who was approaching 80 years of age, rose to the occasion by simply taking out her dentures and painting her face green. That, coupled with a mole or two on her cheek, made her the scariest witch of the night.

Of these four houses, only two—the Ackmans and the Bartosavages—had any Butterfinger bars remaining from Halloween. The ones they had left over were tested for rat poison, but those tests all came back negative. As for the Claxtons, they claimed to have treated visitors with many other items—M&Ms, Hershey's, and Mars bars, among others. As for Mrs. MacDonald, she was known to be the least generous of all the neighborhood stops, and she only had licorice and salt-water taffy, which some trick-or-treaters suspected had been left over from the previous year!

One question that puzzled the investigators was that there had been two other girls who paraded through the neighborhood just before the ghost came. The first had been dressed as Mary Poppins. The second—wouldn't you know it—came dressed as a cheerleader. And both of them were trying out for the cheerleading team in real life. The existence of these two girls threw a monkey wrench into the entire investigation, because it wasn't clear whether the ghost had been singled out, or whether the killer would have been happy to knock anyone off just to create one more space on the squad.

However, Inspector Forsooth thought it extremely likely that the ghost had in fact been singled out of the crowd. Acting on that assumption, he was able to identify the perpetrator.

1) Who killed the ghost?

2) How could the killer feel confident that no one other than the intended victim would be killed by the poison?

3) How did the killer's choice of costume play a role?

INSPECTOR FORSOOTH ANSWERS YOUR QUESTIONS

Q1. Was the victim still wearing her costume when she died?

No, she was not wearing her costume.

Q2. How did the killer know who the ghost was?

The killer found out through the grapevine, meaning that there was discussion about who was dressing up as what, so the ghost's identity was known in advance.

Q3. Was there anyone else dressed as a ghost that night?

Not in that neighborhood, no.

Q4. How did they know she would pick that particular Butterfinger bar?

It was the only Butterfinger bar there!

Q5. Did any of the people in the suspect houses

know that the victim was coming by?

No. They had no idea who was coming until they got there.

Q6. Does the fact that the ghost left her friends to go alone have any significance?

Yes, it is quite significant. Had the ghost not gone out alone, there could never have been any assurance that she would pick up the tainted bar.

Q7. Was it important that the ghost was one of the last trick-or-treaters?

It sure was.

Q8. Did the ghost choose her own candy, or was it handed to her?

Great question. The ghost chose her own candy.

Q9. Were Butterfingers the victim's farorite candy bar?

No, they weren't necessarily her favorite, but they were certainly preferable to other choices.

Q10. So the widow, who had bad candy, wanted the cheerleader dead, and she put a good candy in the bad candy?

I didn't say that! What motive could she possibly have had?

Q11. What do Mrs. MacDonald's teeth have to do with it?

Well, remember that the killer wasn't taking any chances that the poisoned Butterfinger bar might end up in the wrong hands or mouth.

Q12. Did the Mary Poppins carry an umbrella?

Sure did. And you're on the right track, but it looks as though you have to dig a little deeper.

 Can you solve the mystery?

 pg. 224

CURIOUS QUANDARIES

GUNFIGHT AT THE OK MOTEL

Hy Conrad

Jack Bosco entered the O.K. Motel office to settle his phone charges and return the key. "You see it on the news? Two guys just robbed a bank here in town and drove off with a million in cash. I guess they'll catch 'em. They got the roads blocked."

The motel manager grunted and printed out a receipt. He watched as the burly traveling salesman walked out the door, nearly colliding with two men who were just coming inside to register. The newcomers said little, kept their heads down, and seemed in a hurry to get a room, even though it was only 11:30 A.M.

At high noon, the shot rang out, a single gunshot. Since only one unit was occupied, the manager didn't have any trouble telling the 911 operator where to send the police.

The responding officer recognized the car in the motel lot from the APB and called for backup. Within minutes six patrol cars were on the scene, and a captain was shouting through a bullhorn. "Police! You're under arrest. Open the door slowly. Throw out your weapons and come out . . ." Before he could finish, a figure at the picture window broke the glass and sprayed the lot with a spurt of semiautomatic fire.

Twelve officers shot back. Over the next few minutes, they fired dozens of rounds until the shadowy form by the corner of the window no longer seemed to be there. "I don't think he's fired since our first response," the captain mumbled to his lieutenant. "Maybe we should go in."

When they broke down the door, the police found one of the robbers on the floor, dead. A volley of bullets had knocked him off a chair positioned by the window. "Stupid. He should have given up or

hid himself better." The captain stepped around to the other side of the bed. That's when he discovered the second body on the rug, lying on its side facing the bed.

The burly figure had been gagged and loosely tied with sash cords cut down from the blinds. The motel manager identified him as Jack Bosco, the salesman who had checked out just moments before the bank robbers checked in.

The captain examined the cords and shook his head. "Not very good with knots." He looked at the single bullet wound and shook his head again. "Why the heck would they do this? What's the point of having a hostage if you kill him right off?"

The second bank robber was caught a short time

later trying to steal a car from a nearby auto dealership. "After we checked in," he said, "I ran across to the market for food and cigarettes. I didn't take the car, just in case there was a description out. 'Course I didn't know they were plastering the T.V. with the bank's video of our faces and the car and everything else. When I left Buddy, we didn't have a hostage or anything. Honest. All I know is when I come out of the market there's a parking lot full of cops shooting up the place. So I just ran."

"Where's the rest of the money'" the captain snapped.

"What rest of the money? It's all in the room. Four big bags of it."

"No, it's not. Only two bags are there. What did you do with the other two?"

"Honest. I just went to the store. A half-hour later, there's a shoot-out and a dead hostage and half the money gone? I don't know what happened."

A short time later the police discovered the whereabouts of the missing bags.

Q. Whodunit? (1) What happened in the motel room? (2) How did half of the money end up where it did? (3) Who killed Jack Bosco?

EVIDENCE *(This case can be solved in 3 clues.)*

Buddy's Autopsy Report

Eighteen 9-mm bullets were recovered from the head and shoulder area, six potentially fatal. One 9-mm wound in central abdomen, also potentially fatal. From the amount and location of blood on the deceased's clothing, it can be deduced that the abdomen wound occurred first.

Jack Bosco's Autopsy Report

Death was caused by a single 9-mm wound to the chest. The lack of abrasions on the wrists and ankles indicate that the deceased either made little effort, or was given little time, to try to loosen the sash cords tied to his hands and feet.

Crime Scene Report

Four weapons were recovered from the room. A hunting knife with "Buddy" carved in the handle. Two semiautomatic .38 caliber rifles, one with a full clip, the other with twenty-one rounds fired. Twenty-one shell casings found on floor by window. Six full .38 clips found on the bed. One 9-mm handgun, five rounds in the clip along with one empty casing. No other 9-mm rounds or clips on site.

Blood samples were recovered from three locations on the carpet, behind the bed, by the window, and just inside the door.

Jack's Car (Miscellaneous Searches)

Glove compartment: A box of 9-mm shells.

Trunk: Suitcase containing personal possessions. Sample case containing ladies' lingerie. Two bank bags, each containing a quarter of a million in $100 bills.

Investigation of Jack's Past (Research)

An inquiry into Jackson Bosco's past reveals a

Colorado Springs, Colorado, arrest record dating from 3 years ago. He had two separate counts of drunk and disorderly, one count of assault, and one count of resisting arrest. All counts were dropped.

Further investigation reveals no prior contact between Bosco and the men suspected in the Planters' National Bank robbery.

Analysis of Evidence

To get a handle on the case, we have to pay attention to the guns. Both men were killed with 9-mm bullets. This rules out the .38 semiautomatics in the robbers' possession. It rules in the police assault weapons and the 9-mm handgun. The weird thing about the handgun is that no extra rounds were found in the room, even though the robbers were well supplied with other ammo. A box of 9-mm shells was found in Jack's car; so, we may speculate that the handgun belonged to Jack.

Since only his head and shoulders were visible above the windowsill, it seems improbable that Buddy would be hit in the stomach by a police bullet. The blood stain by the door also seems odd.

Given this evidence, the money in Jack's car, and his violent, impulsive history, he can no longer be considered just an unlucky hostage.

 pg. 226

SWALLOWING THE GUN

Hy Conrad

May 12, 1:25 P.M.: The police arrive on the scene of what appears to be a grisly suicide. Inside a small, two-story office building lies the body of Hank Bridger, private investigator. Hank had apparently sat down at his desk and shot himself in the mouth. The officers seal the site and then talk to witnesses, beginning with Ethel, the deceased's secretary.

"Hank was out on a case. He came in about noon. I was in his inner office, spraying his plants for bugs. He never takes care of them, and I get tired of looking at the aphids. Anyway, Hank told me to go to lunch and be back by 1:00. Seems he had a lunch appointment of his own at 1:00.

"I had a burger at a fast-food place and did a little window shopping. I was just heading back to the building a few minutes past 1:00. That's when I heard it. Sounded like a truck backfiring. Hank's office is on the first floor; so, it was probably less than 3 minutes from the time I heard the shot until I walked in. When I opened the door to his inner office, I saw him right away, just the way he is now, fallen back in his chair, the gun lying in his hand."

The rest of the story is filled in by another tenant, Blake Barlow, an accountant. "First you have to understand. The four of us own this building. The four tenants are Hank and me on the first floor, Dr. Russell and Milton Engels, a lawyer, on the second. We run the building as a corporation with Hank as the president. Naturally, I do the books.

"Well, recently I ran across something that didn't smell quite right. It looked like one of the corporation members had embezzled quite a decent sum from our escrow fund. Very cleverly embezzled, although I could be wrong. A little past noon today I gave Hank a call. I told him what I'd found. I told

him I needed some papers from his safe to check out my suspicions. I said I would drop by to pick them up when I left the office today about 5:00."

Blake gazes down at the body. Hanging on the coat tree by the desk is Hank's empty shoulder holster. Beside it is a paper shredder that had disgorged several sheets of incomprehensible confetti. "I guess that settles it," Blake says. "Hank was the thief. After my call, he opened his safe, destroyed the papers, then sat down and shot himself."

An old lieutenant is taking notes. "Did you tell any of the other partners about your suspicions?"

"No. Just Hank. He said he couldn't believe one of us would do something like that. He even got insulting about my bookkeeping. I guess he was trying to bluff me into ignoring it. But I wouldn't. So, he killed himself."

The initial investigation points to the same conclusion. There are no bruises or signs of a struggle. Powder burns on the victim's face support the theory that Hank had opened his mouth willingly, wrapping it around the gun barrel. "Maybe he was asleep in his chair, snoring, and the killer caught him unawares," the lieutenant suggests.

"No," says Ethel. "You see, this office is equipped with an electric-eye alarm system. As soon as someone enters either room, an annoyingly loud bell goes off. That would've woke him instantly. He's a light sleeper. Uh, that's what his wife tells me."

Engels, the lawyer, offers his opinion. "No one in his right mind would sit by while someone took a gun and stuck it into his mouth. Has to be suicide."

The lieutenant shakes his head. "Looks bad, all right. Especially since the rest of you weren't even aware of Mr. Barlow's suspicions. But I knew Hank from his old days on the force. I can't believe he'd steal and I can't believe he'd kill himself. There's got to be another explanation."

Q. Whodunit? (1) How did the embezzler know he or she was in danger? (2) Who killed Hank Bridger? (3) How did the killer manage to shoot Hank in the mouth with his own gun?

EVIDENCE (*This case can be solved in 3 clues.*)

Crime Scene Report

Wastebasket contains two pieces of unopened junk mail.

Joke-a-Day desk calendar reveals the date, May 13. Handwritten on the page is the following: "Lunch-Milton-1. Meet here."

Victim's prints are recovered from the safe, the corporation files, and the gun barrel. Partial print of victim's right forefinger lifted from trigger.

Autopsy Report

No undigested food found in stomach. No trace of tranquilizers, depressants, or other sleep-inducing substances found in stomach or blood analysis.

Urine normal. No organ damage.

Minutes traces of phenothiazine, an insecticide, found in blood samples. Not nearly enough to be toxic.

Medical Guide to Poisons (Research)
Phenothiazine (cont.), p. 237:

Symptoms: Contact with this substance in its liquid or gas state commonly results in irritation to the respiratory tract. In large amounts, it can cause liver and kidney damage. Large doses also result in falling blood pressure, darkened urine, impotence, and muscle damage. Convulsions and disturbances in cardiac rhythm have been known to occur, but not in every case.

Ethel's Statement (Affidavit File)
Under intense questioning, Ethel admitted to having an affair with the deceased. "Just a fling last fall. We saw each other for a month and it ended by mutual consent. I half expected him to fire me, but we managed to maintain a working relationship."

Ethel's alibi is corroborated by the two other women working in the building. While window shopping, Ethel ran into the lawyer's secretary and the doctor's nurse. The three of them walked back to the building and were together when they heard the gunshot.

Partners' Alibis (Affidavit File)

All three of Hank's partners claimed to have been alone in their offices between 12:30 P.M. and the time of the shot. The doctor's nurse and the lawyer's secretary went out to lunch together at noon. Barlow himself had recently fired his secretary and not yet replaced her. Occasionally, the partners joined each other for lunch, but today all three claimed to be alone in their offices. Telephone records verify Barlow's call to the deceased at 12:09 P.M.

Analysis of Evidence

Since the victim's prints are on the safe and the folder, it's reasonable to assume that Hank had been curious enough about Barlow's theory to fetch the pertinent documents and look them over. And since today's page has been torn off the calendar and is not found in the wastebasket, it's also reasonable to assume that the killer had lunch scheduled with the deceased today and removed the page containing a note of this appointment.

Next comes the autopsy report. The traces of insecticide were minimal, but the old lieutenant did his homework nonetheless. He discovered that the only symptom Hank might have suffered from after his exposure to the insecticide was a sore throat. A sore throat? Hmm.

 pg. 227

PUZZLE NO.9

A fter beating Watson quite convincingly at Chess, Holmes cleared the board and placed a Rook (Castle) on one of the four center squares.

"The problem with you, Watson, is that you don't think. You must learn to activate your mind," he said. Holmes then pointed to the Rook. "For example, what is the minimum number of moves this Rook needs to make in order to pass over all the squares on the board and then return to its original square?"

Watson could not find the answer. Can you?

(Hint: A Rook can move any number of squares forwards or sideways, but not diagonally.)

 pg.239

THE LAST OF THE
ROYAL BLOOD

Hy Conrad

The limousine pulled through the gates. The three passengers gazed out at the guards with their dogs patrolling the imposing estate. "Cool," Mary Ann whispered. "You become pals with some dude on the Net and you've got no idea that he's really some deposed Middle Eastern shah."

Mary Ann, Chuck, and Rodney were, like the Shah of Ibabi, all in their mid-twenties. All four had become friends on the Internet, but they hadn't thought of meeting until the shah revealed his identity and asked them to visit his home-in-exile on the shores of a Vermont lake. They met for the first time

at the airport when the shah's driver picked them up.

It had been a nearly snowless winter, but the air was still bitterly cold. Rodney pressed his nose to the frosty glass as the mansion came into view. "Poor guy. Parents dead. Stuck out in the boonies with nothing but a male entourage. No wonder he invited us to celebrate his birthday."

Chuck scratched his head. "Why do you suppose he keeps his birthday a secret?"

"I don't think it's a secret. He just maintains a low profile. You know. Keep himself out of the papers, that sort of thing. He's got political enemies. You guys both bought him a nice present, I hope. Like we talked about?" Rodney asked.

Ali, the shah's chief aide, met them at the door and

led them into the grand hall, a room richly decorated, with hundreds of reminders of the owner's desert home. "Thank you for coming. His Majesty looks forward to meeting you. In the meantime, please make yourselves at home." For the rest of the afternoon, they settled into their rooms, recovering from their flights and roaming the eerily deserted mansion.

The shah was overjoyed to meet his electronic pen pals. But even though they had logged on hundreds of hours with him, they felt ill at ease and spent much of the dinner asking about his former kingdom. For dessert Ali brought in a cake, and the three guests unveiled their presents.

Chuck had brought a gift pack featuring delicacies from his home state. "You always ask me about Utah; so, I thought I'd bring you a few things."

Rodney's present was wrapped in leftover Christmas paper. "It's the best book on surfing the Internet," he explained, a little embarrassed by his makeshift packaging.

Mary Ann's gift was tied in paisley silk, pulled

through a gold ring at the top. "It's an Ibabi antique I found in a shop, though I don't suppose you need any more."

The shah unwrapped a small iron statue with a square base. "No, no. This is beautiful. Thank you." He put down his last present, then gazed out at the frozen lake and the lights of the quaint village on the far shore. "It means much to me to finally have friends here. Tomorrow we will talk." And sadly, the young former ruler left the table and headed up to his room.

That night, Ali couldn't sleep. They had never had strangers in this house, and although a security firm had checked their backgrounds, he still felt uneasy. At a few minutes past midnight, the aide walked by the shah's room, tried the knob, and found it unlocked. "Your Majesty?" He opened the door.

The Shah of Ibabi lay faceup across the rug, the handle of an ornamental dagger sticking out of his chest. Ali raced over to the button by the bed and sounded the alarm. A dozen deadbolts flew into place and the mansion was sealed off.

Although it was late, none of the guests were in their rooms. Ali tracked them down and gathered them together in the grand hall. The security director had already phoned the police. In the meanwhile, Ali was determined to find the killer and administer his own kind of justice. He figured he had at least half an hour before the American authorities arrived and took over. He had to move fast.

Q. Whodunit? (1) Who killed the Shah of Ibabi? (2) Why? (3) How was the killer planning to get away?

EVIDENCE (*This case can be solved in 3 clues.*)

Grand Hall (Miscellaneous Searches)

On the wall beside the grand hall fireplace, an ornamental dagger is missing from an arrangement of traditional weapons. On the top surface of a tile display shelf, beside a row of Ibabi carvings, Ali notices a patch of rust about 5 inches square.

Mud Room (Miscellaneous Searches)

A utility room often found at the rear of New England homes, a mud room is used for storage of coats and outdoor gear and as an informal entrance. A search of this mud room produced these items: four pairs of skis and ski poles, four pairs of ski boots, sizes 9 to 11. Four pairs of snowshoes, sizes 9 to 11. Assorted coats, hats, scarves, heavy socks, and gloves, including those of all three guests. Five pairs of ice skates, sizes 6, 9, 9 1/2, 10, 11.

Crime Scene Report

When Ali discovered the body, it was warm to the touch, the blood around the wound still quite liquid. The shah was in pajamas and a robe. There was no sign of forced entry or of a struggle. A lamp beside the shah's reading chair was turned on. A book lay open on the end table beside a cup of warm mint tea.

Guests' Alibis (Affidavit File)

According to their statements and the testimony

of the servants, the guests had been in these locations at the time they were informed of the shah's murder.

Rodney: In the rose garden, getting a little fresh air. The small garden directly behind the mansion is the only part of the grounds safe from the guards and their dogs.

Chuck: On the roof above the tower room, the shah had installed a telescope. Chuck was here on the mansion roof, looking at the stars.

Mary Ann: In the first-floor kitchen, in search of a midnight snack.

Guests' Luggage (Miscellaneous Examinations)

Chuck's luggage: In addition to the usual clothing was the *Book of Mormon*, and *Murder Impossible*, an anthology of mystery stories.

Rodney's luggage: In addition to the usual, one diamond stud earring, driver's license showing Rodney with a moustache, the latest issue of *PC Magazine*, and the book *A Cultural History of Ibabi*.

Mary Ann's luggage: In addition to the usual,

one large, gold hoop earring, and paisley blouse, same pattern as her gift wrapping. No reading matter.

Analysis of Evidence:

None of the guests knew the shah or were related to him; so, the only possible motive is political assassination. Since the assassin probably didn't want to hang around, we can assume that Ali's discovery of the body so soon after the murder interrupted the assassin's flight plans. Escape routes would be limited. The lack of snow precluded skiing to safety while the guards, dogs, and fences would discourage most land-based escape.

The guest luggage gave Ali some food for thought. The solo hoop earring seems like an odd thing for Mary Ann to pack. And a comparison of their reading material, while revealing nothing about motive, might shed some light on the killer's plans.

The clues from the grand hall both seem significant. The missing dagger must undoubtedly be the murder weapon. And the small, rusty square on the tile shelf shows that a metal object had been standing there but was now missing.

 pg. 229

DEATH OF A DUMMY

Hy Conrad

Agent Gleason answered the doorbell and warmly ushered the three friends into his apartment. "There's no water, I'm afraid. Water-main break this whole side of Prague. I had just enough of the bottled stuff to make coffee." The four intelligence officers were officially assigned to the U.S. Embassy. Once a week they met socially for drinks, dessert, and—not poker, that was too uncerebral a pursuit— contract bridge. The evenings were rotated among their homes in the old section of Prague, as was the responsibility for dessert.

Gleason's guests accepted the lack of water with humor. Levy contributed the expected bathroom jokes, then unveiled a cake topped with red marsh-mallow frosting and a candied cherry. "My wife made it; so, no cracks."

"I thought it was my week," Morales said, placing a bag on the counter. "I bought some Czech pastries, Gleason's favorite. What am I saying? He'll chow down anything. Hey, congratulations, Gleason, if I haven't said it before."

The heavyset Gleason had just been promoted to Internal Security. This secretive branch had the directive to root out moles and counterspies throughout Eastern Europe, still a hotbed of espionage despite the end of the Cold War. Morales himself had been up for the post and competition had been fierce. "So, did you get briefed yet?" Morales teased. "You know, all those telltale ways of ferreting out moles: vaccination scars, dental work, old tattoos."

Levy was the director of Internal Security and put an end to the shoptalk. "That's on a need-to-know basis. Let's play. Dessert and coffee after the first rubber."

The fourth player, Paterno, was Gleason's best

friend, in or out of the embassy. Gleason and Paterno grabbed beers from the refrigerator and sat down to play against Levy (scotch on the rocks) and Morales (coffee, black). In keeping with their routine, the bridge table was set up with one deck instead of  the usual two, giving them a little more time between hands.

The cards fell evenly and the first rubber took over an hour. At some point in the proceedings each of the four men was dummy, the nonplaying partner. In each case, the dummy took advantage of his break, getting up to stretch his legs or refill his drink. Morales had just warmed up his coffee and picked up another beer for Gleason when Levy put down his cards with a frown. "These are sticky. Time for a new deck."

Gleason, the host, gathered up the old cards, dropped them into a wastebasket, then went and fished around in a sideboard drawer. "Here we are. I knew I had one." Gleason tossed the unopened box to Paterno, who unwrapped it and began to shuffle.

Gleason stretched his arms and wandered away from the table. A minute later, just as he was crossing back to join the others, the overweight agent began to breathe heavily. Sweat dripped from his brow. He swayed, then collapsed to the floor. Special Agent Gleason was dead.

Despite their familiarity with death, the three agents couldn't believe the obvious signs. For several minutes, they tried reviving the dead man. Finally, following a nasty hunch, Levy bent down over the corpse of his newly appointed assistant and smelled his breath. "Cyanide," he muttered.

"Cyanide?" echoed Paterno. "That's impossible. How? What the heck was he eating?"

"Are you kidding?" Morales said. "Gleason? The human vacuum? God only knows what he's been munching."

Paterno pushed Levy aside and vainly tried to resuscitate his friend. "Must be a heart attack. It can't be . . . I mean, if it's cyanide, then that means one of us . . ." He left the sentence unfinished.

"Yes," agreed Morales with startling frankness. "Either it's suicide or one of us."

Q. Whodunit? (1) Who killed Agent Gleason? (2) How was the poison administered? (3) What clue fingers the killer?

EVIDENCE (*This case can be solved in 3 clues.*)

Autopsy Report

Death was caused by sodium cyanide and probably occurred within one to three minutes of ingestion. Even for someone of the deceased's size and weight, as little as four grains could have been effectively used. An undissolved granule of sodium cyanide was discovered stuck between two left molars and indicates the poison had been administered in granular form rather than dissolved in a solution.

Levy's Testimony

"I basically knew Gleason from our weekly bridge games, not much more. He'd just been promoted to my department, Internal Security, but hadn't yet started. Paterno and Gleason were best friends. They regularly took vacations together, usually to the Adriatic beaches with girlfriends. Morales and Gleason had been rivals for this new job, but that's no reason to kill anyone. Why was Gleason chosen over Morales? I suppose the main reason was dedication. Gleason seemed more dedicated to the 'firm.'"

Search of the Kitchen

The presence of seven identical Czech pastries and a single empty doily point to the possibility that the deceased ate the eighth. The field of red marshmallow icing covering the cake appears undisturbed. The dish towel seems slightly sticky. Pastries, cake icing, towel, beer bottles, and glasses were all removed for testing.

A small, crumpled glassine envelope was found

in the kitchen trash. Interior is coated with minute granular residue (white). Removed for testing.

Analysis of Food and Drink

Samples taken from beer bottles, glasses, dish towel, cake icing, and pastries. Tested for hydrogen cyanide and derivatives. Minute traces of sodium cyanide discovered on dish towel. Other results all negative.

Examination of the Gard Table

A half-dealt deck of playing cards is found on the table. Many fronts and backs are slightly sticky. A playing card box is near the table center. Four coasters, no ashtrays, scoring pad, and pencil. All beer bottles, empty or full, were taken in for testing as was the pencil lead.

Analysis of Evidence

Due to lack of an obvious motive, the best approach might be to concentrate on the physical evidence first.

The poison took effect in one to three minutes, logically placing the victim in the kitchen at the time of ingestion. A granule was found in his teeth, indicating that the poison had not been dissolved in a liquid. Since no cyanide was discovered in any foodstuffs, it's probable that the victim ate the only tainted item. This eliminates the identical minipastries, since the killer had no way of knowing which one the victim would filch. The presence of cyanide traces on the dish towel leads to the assumption that either the killer or victim wiped his hands on the towel after touching the poison.

The sticky cards present an interesting problem. How did the cards get sticky?

A. pg. 231

PUZZLE NO.10

Sherlock Holmes arrested the butler of the Westwood mansion for poisoning the entire Westwood family. After confessing, the butler went on to explain to Holmes just exactly how it was done. He filled a wineglass half full of wine, and another glass twice the size one-third full of wine. He then topped up each glass with poison before pouring the contents of both glasses into an empty wine decanter.

Can you deduce how much of the mixture is wine and how much is poison?

A. pg.239

THE DAY OF THE DEAD

Hy Conrad

In the cool, pine-forested foothills southeast of
Mexico City lay Hacienda del Sol. The estate was
austere and proper yet somehow hospitable, much
like its owner, Maria Monteneras. Maria, a national
institution, was a multimedia earth mother, author
of books like *Frugal Hospitality* and star of her own
television series, "Entertaining with Mama Maria."

When Maria's beloved husband, Pepe, died, all
Mexico grieved. It happened one night, after a small
dinner party. A drunken Pepe Monteneras fell from
a footbridge on the hacienda property and was
dashed to death in the dry riverbed below. Rumors
of suicide and murder circulated in the tabloid press,

then quickly faded. A full year after Pepe's accident, Maria finally came out of her mournful seclusion.

Roberto Robles was Maria's agent and friend. He and his wife arrived Friday afternoon. They unpacked in one of the guest rooms, then strolled among the dusty olive trees. "How like Maria to mark her return to life with a weekend party," Inez Robles said in hushed admiration. Roberto grunted and frowned. "What's the matter with you?"

"Tomorrow's the Day of the Dead," Roberto said, referring to the Mexican observance of All Souls' Day. "It was exactly one year ago tomorrow that Pepe died. Why did she invite us?"

"She didn't want to be alone."

Roberto still frowned. "You, me, Hugo, Yolanda. We were all here last year, this same weekend. And now Maria invites us back, the same four who were here when Pepe died. I wonder . . ."

Hugo and Yolanda were sitting in the hacienda's homey kitchen also wondering. "I don't know why Maria took it all so hard," Hugo hissed a bit maliciously. "Everyone knew Pepe was philandering about. I'm surprised he died a natural death, what with jealous husbands, perhaps a mistress fed up with his promises . . ."

"Sh!" Yolanda warned her husband just in time. "Maria, dear. I can't believe you're entertaining a house full of guests all by yourself."

"Mama" Maria breezed into the kitchen. "As my publisher, you should know my methods, Yolanda." She was at the counter, already beginning to chop garlic. "Inez is a vegetarian. Hugo eats fish at every dinner; no red meat. Roberto has a milk allergy. If you plan ahead, being a good hostess isn't any more time-consuming or expensive.
As for servants . . . Well, tomorrow is a holiday." She paused, cleaver poised in midair. "A day to remember our loved ones."

That evening, true to form, Maria served up a seemingly effortless feast. They were still laughing and talking long past midnight when Maria made the final toast. "To old friends, here and gone." She drank. "And now I must marinate tomorrow's dinner. Please enjoy yourselves." And she vanished into the kitchen.

Of the four guests, Inez rose earliest on Saturday morning to find breakfast pastries and strong coffee already brewing. A note on the stove announced, "I'm working in the cottage this morning. You all know where to find what you need. Perhaps this afternoon we'll go horseback riding. Maria."

By noon everyone was up and wandering the grounds. By two, they were growing restless. "I told her she had to finish the new book," Yolanda whined. "But I didn't think she'd do it on a holiday."

By three they were worried. Hugo and Roberto walked over to the work cottage. Even from a distance, through the pulled window curtain, they recognized the silhouette sitting at her writing table. "She's been in that same position for hours," Hugo said as he knocked. "Something's wrong." There was no answer.

Neither man knew what to expect when they broke down the cottage door. They certainly didn't expect to find what they did, a room empty except for a mannequin. The store dummy wore one of Maria's trademark wigs and was propped up in her chair.

The guests immediately set out to search, calling Maria's name at the top of their lungs. Yolanda was crossing the foot bridge when she happened to remember Pepe's accident a year earlier. Reflexively, she glanced down into the dry riverbed below, then screamed.

Maria's lifeless, bloody body lay on the sun-bleached rocks. "Just like Pepe," Yolanda muttered to herself. "The Day of the Dead."

Q. Whodunit? (1) Who killed Maria Monteneras? (2) What was the motive? (3) Maria accidentally left a clue pointing to her killer. What was it?

EVIDENCE (*This case can be solved in 2 clues.*)
Suspects' Actions and Alibis

At 1 P.M., the time when the attack presumably took place, all four suspects claimed to be in different areas of the estate. None of their alibis can be corroborated.

At the policía's request, all four suspects remained at the hacienda. On Saturday, Yolanda barbecued the three Argentinean beefsteaks left marinating from the night before. For herself, Inez grilled the prepared vegetables left in the refrigerator. For dessert there were three custard flans and a chilled fruit compote for Roberto. Even in death, Maria was the perfect hostess.

Note Found at the Scene

"Meet me on the footbridge at 1 P.M. Don't let anyone see you. And bring this note. I'll explain when you arrive." (unsigned)

The above was found in thc pocket of the dress Maria was wearing. The writing is not yet identified, but it matches the handwriting on the note Maria supposedly left in the kitchen.

Scene of the Crime

Maria Monteneras had fallen through a hole in the bridge's wooden railing. An examination of the broken edges shows that it had been sawed nearly through. A simple push would have been enough to break the railing.

The victim's clothing was torn.

Autopsy Report

"A preliminary examination places the time of death between noon and 2 P.M. on Saturday. Scratches on the arms and face attest to a struggle having taken place between the victim and her attacker."

Examination of Victim's Bedroom

In a locked bottom drawer, the police found a pile of canceled checks, all signed by Maria. The checks had all been made out to Confidential Results, a Mexico City firm of private investigators. The first was dated December 8, eleven months earlier. The checks were dated in regular intervals from

December through late September. Also found was a small manila envelope labeled with the notation "please return." Inside the envelope was a hand-carved button with torn threads attached.

Analysis of Evidence

On the day before the murder, Hugo made a good point. Plenty of people, men and women, could have motives for killing Maria's late husband.

The location and date of Maria's murder, replicating those of her husband's death, are too great to be labeled a coincidence. Also, the fact that the foot-bridge railing had been sawed through makes this murder seem well planned.

The two notes were either both written by the killer or by Maria herself. Likewise, the mannequin had either been placed at the window by the killer or by Maria. The most logical reason would be to provide an alibi or to disguise the time of death.

As for Maria, several facts seem significant. The weekend party mirroring the party from a year ago, the employment of private investigators, the torn-off button—all these point to the hostess's involvement in some secret plan.

On close examination, Maria's frugal but organized system of entertaining may provide a pivotal clue to her killer's identity.

 pg. 233

THE JUDGE'S JUDGEMENT DAY

Hy Conrad

Guido Sentini entered the downstairs drawing room. His mother glanced up and smiled. "That was very nice, taking up your father's breakfast."

"Ernesto did much of the serving. He knows how Papa likes it. I'm sure he thinks I must want something." The young playboy laughed. It was true, he did want something from his father. But he knew it would take more than a few breakfasts to make thc stern judge part with the 60 million lire young Guido needed to pay off his debts.

The usual Vivaldi concerto poured down the stairs from the judge's second-floor office. "He's working," Yolanda Sentini sighed. Every day was like this, taking care of the estate and the servants while her husband, almost a stranger to her, was either off in the law courts of Naples or here at home, playing the same morning music and reviewing upcoming cases in his office. It was like being a widow, only without the freedom.

Down in the garden, Ernesto and the doctor both heard the Vivaldi. Reflexively, they looked up at Judge Sentini's curtained window and saw his seated silhouette at the desk. "A man of habits is easier to protect," Ernesto mumbled. He was the judge's bodyguard although he often felt like a maid. The government had hired him right after Judge Sentini sent a Mafia don to jail and received his first barrage of death threats.

Ernesto didn't consider his job a difficult one. They were in the Gulf of Naples, on an island with only a few private homes and no town to speak of. Unlike some of Ernesto's previous clients, the jurist followed his instructions to the letter. At night, Judge Sentini and his wife locked themselves into their suite with Ernesto's room right next door. On days when the judge worked at home, he locked himself into his office, as much for privacy as for safety. The alarm was always activated.

The gunshots came during a quiet stretch in the music—three bangs, one right after another, followed by a man's muffled cry of pain or alarm. Dr. Sentini, the judge's brother, glanced from the window to Ernesto, who was already running across the garden, through the hedge maze and toward the house.

It was less than 30 seconds later that Guido Sentini popped his head out of a second-story window. "The office door's locked," he shouted. Ernesto stopped running and was now fumbling for his own key. Guido saw this and shook his head. "No good. Papa left his key in the keyhole. We can't unlock it."

Ernesto's next actions seemed almost automatic. The gardener had left a pruning ladder up against a cherry tree. Ernesto grabbed it, flung it against the house and began to climb. When he reached the ter-

race window, the guard took out his semiautomatic and used the butt end to smash the glass. The sound of a siren screeched through the estate as he reached inside to find the latch and let himself in.

The alarm was still screaming when Ernesto unlocked the office door. Yolanda, Guido, and Dr. Sentini were waiting on the threshold. "He's dead," the terrified guard announced in disbelief.

Yolanda looked past him and saw her husband. The judge was face up on the carpet, three circles of blood emblazoned on his chest. Guido turned his mother away from the sight as Dr. Sentini rushed into the office.

"There's no one in the room," Ernesto stammered. "And no gun."

"Dead," the doctor confirmed as he knelt over

his brother's body. "Guido, get your mother out of here. Ernesto, turn off that blasted alarm and call the police."

Guido and Ernesto did as they were told, returning to the office as soon as they could. The soothing strains of Vivaldi still filled the air. "Don't touch anything," Dr. Sentini said. "I have no idea how any assassin could get in, but we're locking this room until thc police arrive."

They all watched as Ernesto turned the key and took up his post in front of the crime-scene door. He was still there a half-hour later when the Naples police docked at the jetty and raced up to the house, only to be faced with an impossible crime: a locked-room mystery that was to strike fear into the heart of every judge in Italy.

Q. Whodunit? (1) Who killed Judge Sentini? (2) How did the killer get in and out of the locked office? (3) What was the motive?

EVIDENCE (*This case can be solved in 1 clue.*)

Autopsy Report

"Death was caused by three gunshot wounds, each approximately one centimeter in size. Entry points are the right chest wall, the left chest wall, and the sternum. No burn or gunpowder residue is present. Three .45-caliber automatic rounds have been recovered from the body. Death was probably instantaneous.

"A routine examination of body fluids reveals a high concentration of diazepam, a muscle relaxant often sold under the name Valium. Although not administered in a lethal dose, the drug nonetheless would be capable of producing severe muscle weakness, drowsiness, perhaps even a coma. An examination of the stomach contents suggests the diazepam was ingested fifteen minutes to a half-hour before death, probably in conjunction with food."

Search of the Murder Scene

"The body was discovered face up on the carpet, approximately halfway between the desk and the stereo system. The desk chair was found turned over on the floor. The carpet's pile flow indicates the decedent may have dragged himself or been dragged partly across the room. The stereo system was found still turned on, a tape of Vivaldi concerti in the cassette player.

"The suite is comprised of the office itself and an adjacent bathroom. Except for the terrace glass broken by the bodyguard, all windows were locked from the inside, as was the single door to the hallway.

"No firearm was found in the suite."

Chemical Analysis of the Victim's Breakfast

The remains of the decedent's breakfast tray were analyzed. Dissolved traces of diazopam were found in the coffee pot and in the coffee cup.

Search of the Medicine Cabinets

A half-empty container of Valium was discovered in the medicine cabinet of the master bedroom with a pharmaceutical label identifying it as the property of Yolanda Sentini. Signora Sentini admits to being under her brother-in-law's care for nervous distress. The master bedroom suite is locked only at night.

Alibis

Ernesto and Dr. Sentini were together in the far garden. Yolanda Sentini claimed to be in the drawing room drinking coffee—no corroboration. Guido Sentini was in his second floor bedroom, adjacent to Judge Sentini's office—no corroboration. The gardener, cook, and maid were together in the basement kitchen having a late breakfast.

All suspects deny having yelled or cried out in the seconds following the gunshots.

Analysis of Evidence

Everyone in the house had access to the diazepam. The three suspects who could have most easily placed it in the judge's coffee are Yolanda, who brewed it; Ernesto, who arranged the breakfast tray; and Guido, who poured the judge's first cup.

The huge, frightening puzzle of the murder—how an unseen killer could get in, get out, and dispose of his gun without being seen or triggering the alarm—can be broken down into a series of smaller puzzles.

The first is the man's muffled cry heard just after the gunshots. It had to come either from Guido or from the judge himself. Guido denies having made any such sound, and the autopsy indicates that the judge died almost instantly.

The next puzzle involves the dragged body. If the judge dragged himself, then his death was not instantaneous. If, on the other hand, the killer dragged him, he or she must have had a good reason for taking valuable time to do this.

The presence of diazopam in the judge's system brings up the third puzzle. Why? If the killer just wanted to kill, why didn't he or she use a more effective poison? It would have been much less risky than a shooting. Or why not just shoot the judge without the poison? Why were both methods necessary?

A. pg. 235

SOLUTIONS

COUNTRY KILLING—Spinner Webb said he could see through the small crack in the door that the house had been ransacked, yet it was so dark he tripped over his aunt's body. If he could see it was ransacked through the crack, he should have seen the body with the light from the open door. He probably killed his aunt, locked the chain, went out the window, and then broke down the door to set the scene for his story.

SPEEDY GETAWAY—It is unlikely that bank robbers would use such an unusual car unless they planned to get rid of it quickly. The two women could not have seen a dent on the driver's side of a car going the same direction as Dr. Quicksolve because they were at the bus stop on the right-hand side of the road where Dr. Quicksolve had to roll down the passenger window to talk with them. The bearded bank robber who did not speak could easily have been a woman in disguise. Dr. Quicksolve suspected the women ditched the car nearby and told the story about the passing Jaguar to steer the police away from them.

BACKYARD BANDIT—Mr. Dare claims he could hear someone picking a lock above the noise of a lawnmower, and that he saw a man through an eight-foot hedge well enough to describe him.

THE CASE OF THE BULGONIAN SPY— Perry was away from his papers between 9:00 and 9:15. Gulkovo left the bar at 8:45 and did not return to the bar until 9:15. Impalus, however, returned to the bar at 8:45 and could have remained until as late as 9:15. Only he, therefore, had the opportunity to steal the papers.

FAKE OUT—The fact the driver has no identification is very suspicious. It could be the robber and/or Spider himself. Dr. Quicksolve suspected the robber pulled over to look as if he had fixed a flat and had been there a longer time. He could easily and quickly have let the air out of the spare tire to make it flat. If it had just been taken off the car on this snowy morning, however, it would also be wet.

WOOF! WOOF! BANG! BANG!—Sergeant Shurshot suspected Barrie Scarrie and was talking about his picture on his driver's license. Scarrie said he heard the dog bark and two shots. If a stranger had broken in, the dog would have probably reacted to protect his owner and their home. The dog would have been shot first. If a friend, like Scarrie, had been let in, the dog would not have barked until he saw his owner was hurt. Scarrie looked like a serious suspect.

THE TALE OF THE GENEROUS RAJAH—
Morton Henry Stanley was correct in asserting that, if he could know what was in one chest, all of which were mislabeled, he could deduce what was in the other two. Suppose he had succeeded in opening the middle chest, the one with the emerald sign. It would have contained either diamonds or rubies. If it had contained diamonds, then the rubies would have been in the chest with the diamond sign and the emeralds would have been in the chest with the ruby sign. If it had instead contained rubies, then the diamonds would have been in the chest with the ruby sign and the emeralds would have been in the chest with the diamond sign. Only by these combinations could all three chests have the wrong signs. Had he chosen and opened one of the other two chests, similar reasoning would have revealed the contents of all three.

Unfortunately for the good explorer, he failed to notice that the rajah had said that the befuddled servant had failed in each of his attempts to match a sign to the right chest. As Stanwick noticed, there were in fact four such attempts, the first being when the servant put the emerald sign on the first trunk. Only after that did he arrange the signs in their final order (diamond-emerald-ruby). This meant that the first trunk contained neither emeralds nor diamonds. It therefore contained the rubies. Since the second chest had the emerald sign, the emeralds must have been in the third chest, and the diamonds must have been in the second.

The offer of a lockpick was therefore an unnecessary ruse. Stanwick knew this, but Morton Henry Stanley never suspected it.

THE MYSTERIOUS WOMAN—Dr. Quicksolve knew that the Mysterious Woman, a master of disguises, was as tall as Fred at the last party when she was all dressed up including high heels, which would have made her a little taller than she really was. The woman in the room was taller than Fred, so she couldn't be the suspect. The "man," however, without high heels, was the only one in the room who was the right height. She had changed into some of

Fred's clothes and hid her purse when she realized she couldn't escape through the window.

STANWICK VISITS SCOTLAND YARD—
James Malcolm stole the documents.

If he and his wife had gone to the theatre, the ticket-taker would have kept half of each ticket he tore. Thus, when Malcolm carelessly produced both halves of two torn theater tickets, his alibi was proved false.

DEATH OF A CON MAN—Cochran is the killer.
There are several proofs, of which this is one:

The second statements of Cannon and Cochran contradict each other. Therefore one is true and one is false. Since each suspect is making one true and one false statement, the first statement of one of them, denying guilt, is true, and the other denial is false. Thus, one of them is the killer.

The killer cannot be Cannon, since both his statements would then be false. Therefore the killer must be Cochran.

MURDER LAKE—Dr. Quicksolve knew an automatic would spit out empty shells as it was fired. Since he found no shells, he figured Mr. Joyboat did the shooting from the boat. If no gun were found on him or the boat, he probably threw it in the lake.

SMITH AND SMITH, EX-PARTNERS—He wanted to see if Mr. Smith's shoes were wet. If they were, he must have sneaked in the back door to surprise his partner and kill him, and Dr. Quicksolve would have solved another case, because, coming through the garage, they would be dry.

They were. He had. He did.

COOL MICKEY—Mickey could have frozen the poison into the center of the ice cubes. That way he knew the drink would be safe for a few minutes until the ice began to melt. He figured that drinking from her glass and then leaving would give him a great alibi.

RANSOM RESCUE—John wanted a lineup because he knew the girl was blindfolded and wouldn't recognize him. Frank couldn't fool a lie-detector test.

COUNT THE CLUES—1) He left his car unlocked for a quick getaway.

2) As he went into the bank, he checked around for police or anything else that might hinder his getaway.

3) His right hand held the gun in his pocket so it would not bounce around, so no one would notice the outline of a gun in his pocket, and so he could draw the gun quickly.

4) He also wore baggy clothes with his shirttails out to hide the gun in his pocket.

5) A bank robber often wears a baseball cap because the long brim helps cover his face.

6) He also lowered his head to keep his face out of sight of cameras and witnesses.

7) Quicksolve watched the teller's face for any sign of shock or fear as she read the note. This was the strongest clue.

8) The final clue was the large bag of money

which took on special significance because of all the other clues that he had already seen.

THE CASE OF THE EDGEMORE STREET SHOOTING—Kravitz said that Walder was approached from behind and shot before he could see his assailant. If this were true, Walder would have been shot in the back, not in the chest.

Kravitz was convicted of the murder.

A QUIET MORNING AT THE OFFICE—Jasper had cleaned off his desk the previous night, unpacked his papers only after arriving that morning, and kept his work schedule to himself. Once shot, he had slumped over his papers. Only someone who had seen him at his desk before he was shot could have known what he was working on.

Springer, however, had referred to Jasper's working on performance evaluations. He could have known this only by seeing the papers on Jasper's desk that morning before the shooting. Springer had therefore lied about not seeing Jasper that morning before the shooting, which only the killer would have had reason to do.

THE STOCKHROKER'S LAST MORNING—

Golding said Steinberg was seized with convulsions as soon as the coffee cup left his lips, and that no one had been in the room since his death. If this were true, the coffee cup would not have been placed back on the saucer, where Stanwick found it.

Golding had actually entered Steinberg's office from his own office while Steinberg was sipping his coffee and reading the paper in the easy chair. Engaging Steinberg in conversation, Golding slipped poison from the vial into the coffee. Steinberg drank it and died. Golding then (erroneously) replaced the cup, refolded the paper, and put it aside. Wiping his prints from the vial, he put Steinberg's prints on it and put it in the dead man's pocket. He then typed the suicide note (wearing gloves), went back into his office through the connecting door, entered the reception area, picked up the newsletter documents, and enacted his version of the tragedy.

Golding eventually confessed to murdering his mentor to advance his own career.

A NEW YEAR'S DISSOLUTION—If the poison was not administered by food, drink, or inhalation (since no one else was affected), it must have been administered by touch, through the victim's skin pores.

The only thing Dunhope touched shortly before his collapse that he hadn't touched earlier, and that no one else had touched, was the inside of the napkin served with his hors d'oeuvres. (Remember that Miss Schultze was still holding a napkin.) Therefore this had been doctored with poison.

The critical event was Dunhope's being bumped and spilling his Champagne. Since he was not carrying a handkerchief, he must have opened his napkin to clean up the spill and so touched the poison. Only Henson had helped serve the hors d'oeuvres (and napkins) and then bumped Dunhope, causing him to open his napkin. Henson was therefore the logical suspect.

Walker's investigation bore out Stanwick's conclusions. Henson was convicted of murdering his partner to gain full control of their lucrative agency.

THE FINAL FORECLOSURE—1) Who killed Niles Bronson? Graham Moss was the killer, assisted by Herman Gertner.

2) What was the role of the accomplice? To dispose of the murder weapon. After killing Gertner, Moss put the knife in a sheath, placed the sheath in a bag, and dropped it down the trash chute to Gertner, who was waiting on his floor, several floors below, with a basket or some such receptacle to catch it. Gertner later placed the weapon in his bowling bag so he could remove it from the building without attracting suspicion. (Note that Gertner would have been most unlikely to even temporarily survive a plunge of as much as fifteen stories, so one can infer that he lived well below Niles Bronson.

Jeff Carrington and Graham Moss, on the other hand, lived above Bronson.)

Why not Carrington instead of Moss? Well, note that in his journey through the condominium complex, Inspector Forsooth spoke to the security personnel in between speaking to Moss and Carrington. Why? Because Carrington lived in a penthouse apartment (hence the splendid views), which was accessed via a different elevator bank! To get to Bronson's apartment, Carrington would have had to return to the main floor—as Inspector Forsooth did—where he would have been spotted by the ever-vigilant security folks.

By the way, we know that the building had a trash chute by the fact that Rose was taking her garbage out on a Saturday afternoon (NCAA semifinal games are played on Saturdays). It would be highly unlikely for anyone to come around picking it up on a Saturday or a Sunday, and it would also be unlikely that the garbage would remain in the hallway of such an upscale building.

Note that the description of the murder scene

indicates that Bronson was killed before the beginning of the basketball game(s), because his TV was still tuned to FOX ("Tales from the Crypt"), whereas it would have been on CBS had he been alive to watch the basketball. Therefore, neither Moss nor Gertner has any alibi for that time. (I suppose Moss could have changed the channel after killing Bronson to make it look as though he was killed after the games, but Rose Kravitz's intrusion eliminates that possibility.) Finally, the fact that Moss's personal fortunes were turning around is irrelevant. He didn't find out about the accounting firm moving into his building until Monday, by which time Bronson was already dead.

3) Who killed Herman Gertner and why? Either Gertner was trying to blackmail Moss or expose him. Either way, Gertner wasn't cooperating, and Moss decided to get rid of him, too. Case closed.

DEATH AT THE CLINIC—McGowan arrived two and a half hours after Rosella's opened, at 11:30 A.M. He was there half an hour before and after the noon whistle, and so left at 12:30 P.M. Workman arrived 45 minutes later, at 1:15 P.M., and stayed at least half an hour. Since Lola died at 1:44 P.M., he was the killer.

Beard arrived at 2:30 P.M., at the end of an hour-long soap opera that began at 1:30 P.M., found Lola dead, and left.

DEATH COMES TO THE COLONEL—Since the colonel's phone rang, it must have been on the hook. According to George Huddleston, however, the colonel had had a sudden seizure while dialing, and nothing had been touched since. If this were true, the phone would have been dropped, and would not have been found back on the hook.

Huddleston was later convicted of poisoning the colonel for inheritance money.

THE PIANO REQUITAL—1) Who killed Gilbert von Stade? Vivien Frechette. She felt she was every bit von Stade's equal (as evidenced by her strong performance of the complicated piece he had chosen), but she never got anywhere near the recognition he did. That's right: Gilbert von Stade was the victim of professional jealousy.

2) What was the method, and why did it work? Just before the beginning of the show, Frechette laced a couple of the black keys in the upper (right-hand) region of the piano with a combination of batrachotoxin and DMSO (dimethyl sulfoxide, in case you want to impress your friends). Note that she didn't have to go to South America to find the poison; it is available at various medical labs in the United States, for example. And all it took was a few drops.

As discussed in the question-and-answer session, DMSO plays a vital role because of its property of being quickly absorbed into the body. DMSO is capable of carrying other compounds into the bloodstream along with it, even if the person's only contact with the mixture is with the surface of the skin. However, one of DMSO's common side effects is that it leaves the user with a garlicky taste in his mouth! (Note: It was quite unlikely that von Stade's garlic breath came from something he ate. After all, he was in the men's room between the dinner and the performance, and he could have used any of the items there to deal with the garlic taste that he plainly disliked.)

The reason why Heinrich Albertson wasn't killed is that his piece (Etude in C-Major) uses almost no black keys, whereas von Stade's piece (Etude in G-flat) is commonly referred to as Chopin's "black key" etude, such is its emphasis on flats and sharps. Because the poisonous solution was a skimmed-on liquid, von Stade might have noticed that something was amiss, but, being the seasoned professional that he was, he evidently concluded that the show must go on.

In theory, the fact that the show went on would have boded poorly for Vivien Frechette, who followed von Stade in the evening's program. But von Stade had basically wiped the keys clean with his hands; in addition, Frechette's first piece, being slow and melancholy, was much longer than the others, which, coupled with the disruption following von

Stade's death, would have given the remaining solution time to evaporate under the stage lights! These factors all but eliminated the possibility that a lethal or even toxic dosage could have made its way into her bloodstream. (Also, her first piece uses almost exclusively the white keys in the lower ranges of the keyboard, as opposed to the higher-pitched flats and sharps of the black-key etude.)

Theoretically, it was possible that someone who wasn't familiar with the music was trying to kill Heinrich Albertson instead, but the only person who was unfamiliar with sheet music was Marla Albertson; however, she was still very much in love with her husband, and had no apparent reason to do him in. And that's a wrap.

MURDER AT THE CHESSBOARD—Rimbach's story implies that the murder occurred during a game of monochromatic chess. In this form of chess, the knight, a piece that moves only from a black square to a white square or from a white square to a black square, can never move.

In the position on the dead man's chessboard, however, a knight had moved to the center of the board. Rimbach is therefore lying. He committed the murder and then set the scene in the study, but in setting up the chess position made a fatal error.

THE CHURCHILL LETTER—The letter was dated in 1950 and refers to "Sir Winston," but Churchill was not knighted (thereby earning the use of the title "Sir") until 1953.

PIER FOR THE COURSE—1) Who killed Bart Strunk? David Willoughby.

2) Who killed Wayne Metzger? Again, David Willoughby.

3) How was Metzger killed? You must be specific as to how the crime was perpetrated.

The conspiracy was between senior vice president Wayne Metzger and vice president David Willoughby. Metzger pressured Willoughby into shooting Bart Strunk so that he (Metzger) could take over the reins of the company.

But Willoughby insisted on having an alibi. He agreed to shoot Strunk just as he was finishing his caramel apple. The plan was that Metzger would then place the apple core in a cup of water—this would prevent the apple from "aging," as it would if left in the air, and would make it seem as though Strunk had been shot at a time when Willoughby wasn't in the area. Metzger agreed, the idea being that Willoughby would leave the pier area for a remote site, at which point Metzger would wait a little while before getting help, then would take the apple out of the water to misconstrue the time of the killing and provide Willoughby with an alibi.

The only wrinkle was that Willoughby, standing at a point on the shore, killed Strunk a bit too soon—on purpose! Metzger found that the apple was too big to fit in the cup of water, and he therefore hurriedly ate the rest of it himself! This is precisely what Willoughby had anticipated. He knew he had a chance to kill two birds with one stone (ultimately he felt angry at being Metzger's flunky for so many years), and he had taken the opportunity to place peanut oil on the outside of Strunk's caramel apple at its widest point—when, ostensibly, he was checking Metzger's food to make sure he had a ham sandwich instead of peanut butter and jelly. The taste of the peanut oil was obscured by the caramel, and of course Strunk consumed it without any side effects. But Metzger's intense allergy to peanut oil (a well-known and very serious condition) caused his larynx to tighten up within mere seconds of its ingestion. Metzger had time to place the apple in the water cup, but that's about it. He never made it off the pier.

The final touch was that Willoughby made sure he found the bodies first, confident that the others would be distracted by their own projects. When he arrived with Sharon Sturgis, he saw to it that she attended to Wayne Metzger, so that he could attend to Strunk. Willoughby simply removed the apple from the cup of water, thereby creating the illusion that his alibi depended on.

That's it!

SABOTAGE AT CENTIPORE—The records of the storage room terminal establish that the alteration was done on an outside computer, which required the use of a decryption code. Anyone other than the senior engineers would have had to get the new code through Freedman, who was out sick all that week. Therefore one of the senior engineers altered the disk.

If Miller were the culprit, he would have at least delayed his pretended discovery. The competitor thus selected Donlan or Delaney. Selecting Donlan would have been pointless, however, since he would have needed the cooperation of one of the others. He could not enter the storage room alone, and the location of the disk there would have made it very difficult for him to remove it without the engineer with him being aware of it. The selected, and guilty, engineer is therefore Delaney.

HALLOWEEN HORROR—1) Who killed the ghost? The murderer was the girl who was trick-or-treating in the cheerleader costume. She planted a poisoned Butterfinger bar in Mrs. MacDonald's candy bowl.

2) How could the killer feel confident that no one other than the intended victim would be killed by the poison? First of all, the ghost was the next person heading to Mrs. MacDonald's house. Second, even if the ghost elected not to take the Butterfinger bar (which was clearly the best choice available), it was late in the evening, and it was unlikely that another trick-or-treater would come along. Finally, even if the candy bar had not been selected by the ghost or anyone else, Mrs. MacDonald wasn't going to eat it, just as she apparently didn't eat her taffy. You don't see many octogenarians with dentures sinking their (false) teeth into a chewy candy bar.

3) How did the killer's choice of costume play a role? The cheerleader's costume was complete with a set of pompoms. (Actually, the correct term is "pompon," but it looks like a typo!) These "pompoms" came in handy, because they enabled the cheerleader to hide the tainted Butterfinger as she

reached into the candy bowl. She then buried the bar so that it wasn't completely obvious, but so that the ghost (with sharper eyes than Mrs. MacDonald) would be able to spot it. And the rest is history.

GUNFIGHT AT THE O.K MOTEL—(1) Jack killed Buddy, planning to steal the already stolen money. (2) The police interrupted Jack's getaway. (3) He was killed by a stray police bullet.

If we begin with the assumption that our impulsive, violent Jack Bosco recognized the robbers from the television news, then the rest falls into place. Instead of driving off, Jack watched the bandits sneak the million dollars into their room. He watched and thought. And when one of the robbers left to go shopping, Jack made his move.

With the handgun from his glove compartment, Jack knocked on the motel door, pretending to be the manager. He made short work of the solo robber, shooting him in the stomach. Jack transferred the first two bags of money to his trunk and was about to exit with bags three and four when the patrol car pulled up.

What to do? Jack couldn't leave. Could he bluff his way out as a good citizen who struggled with a criminal and had shot him in self-defense? Well, not with all that money in his trunk.

Jack did the only think he could think of, propping Buddy Brinker's body up in a chair, starting the gunfight, then tying himself up, and hobbling for the safety of the bathroom. It was a risky move, but then he could explain that they were planning to take his car and use him as a hostage. No one would be the wiser. He'd even be a media hero. The only thing Jack didn't take into consideration was the stray police bullet catching him on the way.

SWALLOWING THE GUN—(1) Hank told him the embezzler was Hank's lunch date. (2) Dr. Hubert Russell. (3) Russell examined Hank's sore throat. "Say aah!"

The police focused their investigation on Dr.

Hubert Russell, a general internist. They discovered the doctor's gambling addiction and a 6-month-old bank account with a single large deposit that had been eaten away by many small withdrawals. When asked about the deposit, Russell said that he had a trifecta win at the racetrack. Under intense questioning, he broke down, confirming what the lieutenant already suspected.

"Okay, okay," the doctor confessed. "I dropped by Hank's office a few minutes before 1:00. We had a lunch date. He was at his desk looking over some corporation papers. I recognized them at once. Last year's escrow records—right before we changed banks. That's when I fiddled with the books, while we were changing banks. I was going to pay it back. My luck was just about to change. I could feel it. Anyway, Hank told me about Barlow's theory. He didn't believe it for a second, good old Hank. But those papers in his hands were all Barlow would need to start tracing it back to me.

"We kept chatting. All the time I was desperately trying to think of some way to get hold of those papers. Anything I did was just going to arouse his suspicions. And then he started coughing. All of a sudden Hank had gotten a sore throat. He figured he was coming down with a cold and asked me to take a look. People are always asking for free advice."

Russell smiled. "A doctor tells you to open your mouth and you don't think twice. Then, when he's an inch from your face, he asks you to lean back and open wider . . . About ten out of ten close their eyes and say 'Aah!' until you tell them to stop. Hank's gun was hanging in his holster, a foot away. The temptation was irresistible. Eating the gun, you know, a typical cop suicide. Then he could take the blame for the money. It seemed foolproof. What made you suspect?"

THE LAST OF THE ROYAL BLOOD— (l) "Mary Ann." (2) Hired by the Ibabi government. (3) By skating across the frozen lake.

At the time our story opened, the real Mary Ann Nilson lay dead in her Atlanta home, the victim of an assassin hired by Ibabi to kill the last member of the royal family. Shannon Gibbs had been trying to gain access to the shah for some time. When Rodney began bragging over the Internet about his upcoming visit, Shannon knew this was her chance. She wheedled her way into Mary Ann's apartment, killed the unwitting woman, and took her place.

Shannon had done research on the shah but was unprepared for his birthday celebration. Finding herself without a present, she faked her way brilliantly, taking one of the hundreds of knicknacks from the hall, wrapping it in a scarf, fastening it with an earring loop, and presenting the birthday boy with a statute he already owned. Soon enough someone would discover her trick, but by then the shah would be dead and she would be gone.

Her escape plan was just as clever. Before dinner, Shannon took a pair of ice skates (women's size 6) from her luggage and planted them in the mud room. Right after the murder, she would sneak downstairs, slip on her blades, and skate across the frozen lake to a spot where a car was waiting.

Shannon had just finished tying up her skates when the alarm sounded and the doors automatically locked. She had no choice but to remove them, race into the nearby kitchen, and pretend to be making a midnight sandwich. She would try to brazen it out.

Ali grew suspicious when he noticed that "Mary Ann" had been the only guest to arrive without a book or magazine. She obviously didn't intend to be there long enough to do any reading. But before Ali could fit the pieces together, the police arrived and took all three suspects into custody. The real Mary Ann Nilson's body was discovered the very next morning.

DEATH OF A DUMMY—(1) Paterno, Gleason's best friend. (2) By poisoning the cherry on top of the cake. (3) The sticky cards on the table.

Years ago, Paterno (born Yuri Patrenko) was planted in the CIA. It was arranged for him to have a fellow KGB mole as his examining physician. In this way, Paterno's telltale vaccination scars and dental work went unreported.

Though the Cold War was over, Paterno still worked for Russia. Gleason, who had seen Paterno half-naked on various beaches, was about to be briefed on the details of such marks and would have connected this information to his friend.

Paterno brought the cyanide, knowing that Gleason was famous for picking at food, especially desserts. When Paterno saw the candied cherry, he knew Gleason wouldn't be able to resist. During his turn as dummy, Paterno filled the pitted fruit with several grains of poison, then replaced it on the marshmallow icing. Paterno's hands were now sticky from the cherry and the icing, but there was no water to wash his fingers. He certainly couldn't lick them. So, he wiped them off as best he could on a dish towel.

When Gleason filched the cherry during his last kitchen visit, he smoothed over the icing with his fingers, leaving no trace of the cherry, then licked his fingers clean.

During their last full hand, Paterno's sticky hands gummed up the cards, leading Gleason to break out a new deck. Paterno was shuffling this new deck when Gleason collapsed. No one else had touched the deck and yet it also proved to be sticky, just like the old one.

The CIA pieced together this scenario and removed Agent Paterno from Prague. His name soon disappeared from their list of active agents.

DAY OF THE DEAD—(1) Hugo. (2) Self-defense and to prevent arrest; either is acceptable. (3) The frugal Maria did not buy fish for Hugo's Saturday dinner, expecting him to be dead by then.

Exactly one year earlier, fate caught up with Pepe Monteneras. Hugo had discovered that his wife, Yolanda, had been having an affair with the over-sexed Pepe. The jealous husband waylaid the drunken Pepe on the footbridge, pushing him to his death.

From the very beginning, Maria suspected murder. But it was a few weeks later, when she found the strange torn-off button wedged in a rock where her husband had fallen, that she hired her private eyes. It took months of investigation, but they finally traced the button to a hand-made jacket Hugo had bought six years before in Acapulco.

Maria had her killer. And he had to pay for his crime in the same way Pepe paid. On the anniversary of Pepe's death, she would lure Hugo to the bridge, then push him through the carefully sawed railing. The mannequin would provide Maria with an alibi. She would sneak back into the cottage by 1:30 at the latest. Everyone would swear she had been in there, working on her book.

But Maria's plan backfired. Hugo was suspicious. As soon as she attacked, he overpowered her, propelling her into the dry riverbed instead.

Maria's lifelong habits of thrift came to her aid after death. She had not expected Hugo to be alive to eat Saturday's dinner. So, there was no reason to buy a good piece of fish that would just go uneaten.

THE JUDGE'S JUDGMENT DAY—(1) Ernesto, the bodyguard. (2) The gunshot sounds were on the Vivaldi tape. Ernesto shot the drugged judge before letting anyone into the room. (3) A paid Mafia assassination.

The Mafia had to make an example of Judge Sentini. A simple poisoning or a simple shooting would not inspire half the fear that an impossible, phantom murder would. Ernesto was paid a lot of money to arrange it, and all he needed from his employers was a duplicate of the judge's favorite Vivaldi tape, one with the sound of three gunshots placed strategically in the middle section.

Ernesto had keys to the office. It was very easy for him to enter one evening and replace the judge's morning tape with the "gunshot" one. The next morning, while preparing the breakfast tray, Ernesto drugged the coffee pot, then left to find himself an alibi witness in the garden.

As always, the judge followed Ernesto's instructions, locking the door and leaving the key in the lock. He drank his coffee and turned on his music, all part of his unvarying routine. When the gunshots sounded on the tape, Judge Sentini was already partly paralyzed from the diazepam. He cried out in alarm and got up to check the stereo. Then he collapsed, dragging himself partway across the floor.

When Ernesto broke the terrace window, he counted on the alarm to cover up the sound of the real murder. He screwed a silencer onto the muzzle of his semiautomatic, killed his boss, then unlocked the door to admit the rest of the household.

The assassin knew it would take at least thirty minutes before the Naples police arrived. This gave him enough time to reenter the study and replace the gunshot tape with the original. This was an especially easy job since he himself was assigned to guard the room.

PUZZLE ANSWERS

Puzzle 1: Library, Study,
Games room, Kitchen.

Puzzle 2: £1 each.
Only three people had visited the
stall—a grandfather, father and son.

Puzzle 3: 31st December

Puzzle 4: The cards reading from left to right
are: Queen of hearts, Knave of clubs, King of
diamonds, Queen of spades and the Ace of
diamonds.

Puzzle 5: Table 1: 2 full, 3 half full, 2 empty
Table 2: 2 full, 3 half full, 2 empty
Table 3: 3 full, I half full, 3 empty
Solution2: Table 1: I full, 5 half full, 1 empty
Table 2: 3 full, 1 half full, 3 empty
Table 3: 3 full, I half full, 3 empty

Puzzle 6: A coffin.

Puzzle 7: Number22
20 (x4), R0 (4), 76 (- 4), 19 (+4),
23 (x4), 92 (4), 88 (- 4) = 22.

Puzzle 8: Joe Jones
(The numbers 23406 306 held up to a mirror).

Puzzle 9:

Puzzle 10: The wine in the smaller glass was one-sixth of the total liquid, while the wine in the larger glass was two-ninths of the total. Add these together to reveal that the wine was seven-eighteenths. Therefore the poison content had to be eleven-eighteenths.